# TESSA KIROS

~ THE RECIPE COLLECTION ~

# TESSA KIROS

~ THE RECIPE COLLECTION ~

MURDOCH BOOKS

# ~ CONTENTS ~

# ~ INTRODUCTION ~

Born in London to a Finnish mother and Greek-Cypriot father, Tessa Kiros grew up in South Africa in a family that cultivated her love of good food and provided her with a rich store of recipes from both sides of the family tree. After spending her twenties working in restaurants in London, Athens and Mexico, and completing a degree in anthropology and sociology, she travelled to Italy to study Italian and learn about Italian food. She met her husband, Giovanni, while in Tuscany and they still live there today with their two children.

Inspired by the recipes and charms of her adopted homeland, Tessa wrote the first of her many cookbooks, *Twelve*, in 2002. Passionate and enthusiastic about her cookbook, she self-published and quickly attracted the attention of her publisher, Murdoch Books. She returned to Italian life as inspiration with her 2012 cookbook, *Limoncello and Linen Water*, a tribute to the domestic traditions and recipes of her Italian family.

Tessa's diverse family heritage and love of travel provided rich material for the eight cookbooks that followed *Twelve*. Some of these capture her visits to countries close to her heart and take readers along for the journey as she explores villages, laneways and local restaurants. Other books draw inspiration from the quiet pleasures of day-to-day family life, and her heritage — expressed through recipes, stories and traditions handed down from past generations.

This collection is a celebration of Tessa's publishing journey to date. It offers a taste of the hundreds of recipes she has written, collected and treasured over the years and reflects her love of many cuisines and cultures. Above all, it highlights her passion for family and good simple food. The recipes have been carefully selected from five of her best-selling books — *Falling Cloudberries*, *Apples for Jam*, *Piri Piri Starfish*, *Venezia* and *Food from Many Greek Kitchens* — and they cover Italian, Greek, Portuguese, South African and Finnish cuisines at their homemade best.

Whether you have well-thumbed copies of Tessa's earlier cookbooks on your bookshelf, or have yet to enjoy her warm and relaxed cooking style, we hope this book opens up a world of recipes, reunites you with old favourites, and introduces you to many, many more.

# ~ GLOSSARY ~

## BRESAOLA

*Bresaola* is cured beef that has been air-dried and salted. It is aged for around two to three months and is usually deep red in colour when you buy it. The top inside round of beef is used for this particular cut, and the end product has a very full, rich flavour. Italians eat bresaola on its own, sliced very, very finely, sometimes with a drizzle of nice olive oil and perhaps a few leaves of rocket (arugula). You can find it in good food stores, delicatessens and some supermarkets.

## CHOURIÇO

This is the Portuguese equivalent of Spanish *chorizo*. It is a cured meat sausage made with pork, fat, paprika and salt. Once the sausages are stuffed, they are dried slowly over smoke, achieving a wonderful smoky flavour that shines through in many Portuguese dishes (like Cozido on page 218). *Chouriço* is often cut open and grilled over a barbecue and can also be flame-cooked with alcohol. Portuguese specialty shops or good delicatessens should have *chouriço*, but you can always substitute with *chorizo*.

## GLISTRIDA

Greens are so important in Greek cooking, and *glistrida*, also known as purslane, is widely used in many dishes. It can be served raw in salads, sautéed and served with meat or fish, or pickled and served as part of a bigger family meal. The leaves are thick and oval, and have a lemony, peppery flavour that add a lot of personality to dishes.

## KASSERI

The Greeks make many beautiful cheeses, some of them so unique that they are protected by law — *kasseri* is one of these. It is made from fresh unpasteurised sheep's milk, but sometimes a little goat's milk is mixed in, too. It is aged for around four months and ends up medium-soft and a little stringy; similar in texture to provolone. Aged *kasseri* is similar to parmesan, so you can always use that as a substitute if you can't get it. In Greece it's used in sandwiches, and also in the fried cheese dish *saganaki* (see page 61).

## KEFALOTIRI

*Kefalotiri* is another cheese that is perfect for making *saganaki*. It is made with a blend of sheep's and goat's milk and very popular throughout Greece and the Greek Islands. Pale in colour, and slightly harder and saltier than *kasseri*, it can be treated in a similar way to parmesan or pecorino and shaved over salads or grated it into sauces and hearty stews for added depth and flavour. It is often mixed with feta and used inside traditional *spanikopita*.

## LINGUIÇA

Similar to *chouriço*, *linguiça* is another Portuguese sausage that is also made with pork, but flavoured with garlic and paprika. It is smoke-cured and makes a good alternative to recipes that call for *chouriço* or *chorizo*. As with those sausages, it can be sliced and fried or grilled, or barbecued and served with other nice meats as part of a bigger feast.

## MIZITHRA

This fresh Greek cheese is made from the milk and whey of unpasteurised goat's or sheep's cheese (and sometimes a blend of both). It is hung in muslin cloths for a few days to drain the whey and a soft, creamy, sweet cheese is left behind (similar in texture to buffalo mozzarella). At this point it can either be eaten as is, or added to dishes and baked. Alternatively, it can be rubbed with coarse salt and hung in muslin for a longer period of time creating a firmer, saltier white cheese that can be grated over dishes to add flavour and character.

## PIRI PIRI

Also known as peri peri, the term piri piri refers to the African bird's eye chilli, which forms the basis for the sauces, marinades and spice mixes that have come to be such a cornerstone of Portuguese cuisine. It comes in many forms: a ground powder, flavoured oil, or as part of a spice mixture that creates piri piri marinade, which adds so much flavour to chicken and meat dishes.

## PRESUNTO

*Presunto* has much in common with its cousin, Spanish jamón. It is produced by dry-curing and hanging legs of ham. Once aged, these legs are then sliced finely and used for the most delicious plates of meat. The type of pig used for *presunto* varies from region to region, and some, such as Chaves in the north of Portugal, claim to have the most delicious *presunto*. It can be bought fairly cheaply in Portugal and is often served as part of a larger meal, or as a snack with some olives and bread.

## TALAGANI

Similar in texture and flavour to haloumi cheese, but slightly creamier and less salty, *talagani* is a traditional handmade cheese from Southern Greece. It's made from sheep's milk and, like haloumi, it is best served sliced, grilled and eaten right away with salads, cooked vegetables or as a side dish to a larger meal. Greek specialty shops may stock it, but if you can't find it haloumi makes a good substitute.

# 1

~ BREAD & BREAKFAST ~

# CINNAMON & CARDAMOM BUNS

These gorgeous buns were always a part of my childhood. They are found everywhere in Finland — and probably all over Scandinavia — in tea rooms and houses. Everyone makes their own and they freeze beautifully so you can just pull out a few when a craving sets in. Don't be put off when you see that the buns need to rise for a couple of hours. You can get the dough together really quickly and then leave it alone without even a glance. The rolling and cutting can be a little tricky the first time you do it, but the second time will be easy.

Put the milk and sugar in a bowl and crumble in the yeast. Leave for 10 minutes, or until the yeast begins to activate. Add the egg, butter, cardamom and salt and mix in. Add the flour, bit by bit, mixing it in with a wooden spoon until you need to use your hands, and then turn it out onto the work surface to knead. It may seem a little too sticky initially, but will become compact and beautifully soft after about 5 minutes. Put the dough back in the bowl, cover with a clean cloth and then a heavy towel or blanket, and leave in a warm place for about 2 hours, or until it has doubled in size.

To make the cinnamon butter, mix together the cinnamon and sugar. Divide the butter into four portions and keep on one side.

Put the dough on a floured work surface and divide it into four portions. Begin with one portion, covering the others with a cloth so they don't dry out. Using a rolling pin, roll out a rectangle, about 30 x 25 cm (12 x 10 inches) and 2–3 mm (⅛ inch) thick. Spread one portion of butter over the surface of the dough with a palette knife or blunt knife. Sprinkle with about 3 teaspoons of the cinnamon mix, covering the whole surface with quick shaking movements of your wrist. Roll up to make a long dough sausage. Set aside while you finish rolling out and buttering the rest of the dough, so that you can cut them all together.

continues on next page …

MAKES 36

**BUN DOUGH**
250 ml (9 fl oz/1 cup) tepid milk
100 g (3½ oz) caster (superfine) sugar
25 g (1 oz) fresh yeast
1 egg, lightly beaten
125 g (4½ oz) butter, softened
2 teaspoons ground cardamom
1 teaspoon salt
650 g (1 lb 7 oz) cake flour or plain (all-purpose) flour

**CINNAMON BUTTER**
2 teaspoons ground cinnamon
50 g (1¾ oz) caster (superfine) sugar, plus 1 tablespoon extra for sprinkling
80 g (2¾ oz) butter, softened
1 egg, lightly beaten

Line two large baking trays with baking paper, or bake in two lots if you only have one tray. Line up the dough sausages in front of you and cut them slightly on the diagonal, alternating up and down, so that the slices are fat 'v' shapes, with the point of the 'v' about 2 cm (¾ inch) and the base about 5 cm (2 inches). Turn them so they are all the right way up, sitting on their fatter bases. Press down on the top of each one with two fingers until you think you will almost go through to your work surface. Along the sides you will see the cinnamon stripes oozing outwards. Put the buns on the baking trays, leaving space for them to puff and rise while they bake. Brush lightly with beaten egg and sprinkle a little sugar over the top.

Leave the buns to rise for half an hour and preheat your oven to 180°C (350°F/Gas 4). Bake them for about 20 minutes, or until they are golden. Check that they are lightly golden underneath as well before you take them out of the oven. Serve hot, warm or at room temperature and, when they are cool, keep them in an airtight container so they don't harden.

# YEASTED MILK BREADS

Some people like these with ham and cheese, but they are also beautiful for breakfast, with butter, jam or marmalade. You will need a large non-stick frying pan — use the closest thing to a baking stone you can find. I love these: they taste like raw cinnamon bun dough for some reason and the sugar feels elusive, almost like a whisper. You can make the dough into one large cake and cut into wedges to serve. They don't keep very well, so either eat them straightaway or freeze them in plastic bags.

Crumble up the fresh yeast (or sprinkle in the dried) into a small bowl, add the lukewarm milk, a handful of the flour and a stolen pinch of the sugar and whisk it all together. Leave until the yeast starts to activate and bubble up a bit. Meanwhile, put the rest of the flour, the sugar and salt in a large bowl and make a well in it.

Pour the foamy yeast mixture into the well with the melted butter and egg, mixing in well with a wooden spoon until you have a soft rough sticky ball. Sprinkle some of the extra flour onto your work surface and, with floured hands, gently knead for a minute or so until the ball is smoothish. (This is a gentle bringing together of the dough without much flour or force.) Put into a large bowl, cover with a tea towel and leave for 2–3 hours in a warm place until it has puffed up well. Line two large baking trays with baking paper.

Divide the dough into about 12 portions, roll them gently into balls with your palms and a little of the flour and put them on the trays, leaving a little space in between. Cover loosely with another sheet of baking paper and a cloth on top of that. Leave to rise for another hour.

Heat up a large heavy-based frying pan or stone to hot then reduce the heat to low. Take each ball of dough (working with four or so at a time depending on the size of your pan). Flatten each ball as smoothly as you can without knocking the air out too much to make a flat disc about 10 cm (4 inches) wide. Dust a little flour on both sides and put into the hot pan over gentle heat. Turn over carefully when the undersides are deep golden (remember they need to have cooked halfway through if they're not to have doughy centres). Cook until the new underside is deep golden and remove to a cloth-lined basket while you cook the others. Cut a cooled one open to check it's cooked.

These are good both warm and cold. Left out they tend to harden and don't keep well, but are great toasted and spread with butter and jam.

**MAKES 12**

25 g (1 oz) fresh yeast or 15 g (½ oz) dried yeast

250 ml (9 fl oz/1 cup) warm milk

500 g (1 lb 2 oz) cake flour or plain (all-purpose) flour, plus a little extra for kneading

150 g (5½ oz) caster (superfine) sugar

2 pinches of salt

40 g (1½ oz) butter, melted and cooled

1 egg, lightly whisked

# HOMEMADE RUSKS

These are what we had in South Africa for breakfast, often dipped in warm milk or coffee. I love having a jar of them in the house always. They are crisp and rustic and beautiful. My friend Sue says her kids always liked to scatter the remaining crumbs over their breakfast cereal.

Preheat your oven to 190°C (375°F/Gas 5). Mix the butter into the flour with your hands or in a blender. Add the sugar, salt and baking powder and then mix in the milk and vinegar until you have a smooth soft dough. Grease a large baking tray with butter and flour.

Roughly divide the dough into three portions. Wet your hands with a little cold water and quickly roll long dough sausages, each about 30 cm (12 inches) long. Your tray needs to be big enough to accommodate them — mine is 34 x 25 cm (13½ x 10 inches) and looks very big when I put the mix on. Arrange the dough rolls parallel on the tray with a few extra dots of butter between them.

Bake for 45 minutes – 1 hour until the tops are golden and crusty. Remove from the oven and turn the heat down to 150°C (300°F/Gas 2). The dough rolls will have joined together but their outlines will still be visible. Cut down their lengths to separate them, then cut each roll into 3 cm (1¼ inch) pieces. Don't touch them for now, leave them on their tray to cool a bit and make them more manageable. Then lift them up and break them in half through their middles so that they look rustic and imperfect. If you find it easier, begin with a knife, chopping through a little and then breaking them apart with your hands.

Return them to the baking tray (lay them on their sides) and the oven for about 30 minutes on each side to dry out a bit. They should be not too toasted, but crumbly and firm. Let them cool completely before storing in a closed container or paper bag, where they will keep well for up to five days.

**MAKES ABOUT 50**

250 g (9 oz) butter, cut into small pieces, plus about 25 g (1 oz) extra

750 g (1 lb 10 oz) cake flour or plain (all-purpose) flour

460 g (1 lb ¼ oz) caster (superfine) sugar

1 teaspoon salt

2 teaspoons baking powder

400 ml (14 fl oz) milk

2 tablespoons white or red wine vinegar

# MIXED BROWN BREAD

I love going to the organic shop and coming out with the various brown paper bags with all the different goods to make this bread. It really makes me feel like I'm doing well when my kids have this for their school sandwiches. Apart from its healthy aspect this is just simply lovely — nice for sandwiches or toasted with butter or jam. You might like to try other flours or combinations, too. This makes one large loaf or two smaller ones, and, if you like, you can easily freeze one and keep it for another moment.

Put the water in a smallish bowl and add the yeast, honey and oil. Stir until the honey melts and then leave it for 10 minutes or so, until it begins to froth up a bit.

Put the farro, buckwheat, rye, wholemeal and bread flours in a fairly large wide bowl and add the linseeds and salt. Toast the sesame and sunflower seeds lightly in a dry frying pan and stir them into the flours.

Add the yeast mixture to the flours and mix through well, kneading it in the bowl for at least 5 minutes until it is elastic. It may still be a little sticky, but only add more bread flour if you can't knead it because it's sticking to your hands. Cover the bowl with a couple of cloths and leave it in a warm and draught-free place for about 1½ hours, or until it has puffed up well. Punch down the dough to flatten it, divide it in half and dust a large baking tray with flour. Shape the dough into two longish loaves and sit them on the tray, leaving space between as they will rise. Make a few slashes on their tops and cover with a cloth, making sure it loops in the middle of the two loaves. Leave it in the same draught-free spot for another 45 minutes or so, until the dough has puffed right up again.

Meanwhile, preheat the oven to 200°C (400°F/Gas 6). Remove the cloth and bake for about 25 minutes, until the bread is golden and crusty all over and sounds hollow when you tap it. Remove from the oven and cool a bit before serving. Best warm or at room temperature.

**MAKES 2 LOAVES**

about 375 ml (13 fl oz/1½ cups) tepid water

20 g (¾ oz) fresh yeast, crumbled, or 10 g (¼ oz) active dry yeast

2 teaspoons honey

1 tablespoon olive oil

120 g (4¼ oz) farro (spelt) flour

100 g (3½ oz) buckwheat flour

80 g (2¾ oz) rye flour

100 g (3½ oz) wholemeal (wholewheat) flour

100 g (3½ oz) bread (strong) flour

15 g (½ oz) linseeds

1 teaspoon salt

40 g (1½ oz) sesame seeds

60 g (2¼ oz) sunflower seeds

# WHITE MILK BREAD OR ROLLS

You can make this as one loaf or shape into smaller rolls. Children love small soft white rolls, it seems. Naturally, you can make different sizes, or a different shape — long are nice for hot dogs. You can easily make a batch and freeze them in small bags, a few together, to whip out at almost the last moment of need.

Put the milk, yeast and honey in a small bowl and stir until the honey melts. Leave it for about 10 minutes, or until it begins to froth a bit.

Put the flour and salt into a larger bowl. Add the yeast mixture, the egg and butter and mix through well. Knead for 10 minutes or so and, if it seems sticky, just hold the bowl firmly and move the dough around with your hand, rather than add more flour. Cover the bowl with a cloth and leave in a warm draught-free place to rise for 1½–2 hours, or until it has puffed up well.

Lightly grease a 30 x 11 cm (12 x 4¼ inch) loaf (bar) tin and dust it with flour. Punch down the dough to flatten it and shape it into a rough loaf of a size to fit the tin. Cover with a cloth and leave in the warm place for another 45–60 minutes, or until it puffs right up in the tin. Meanwhile, preheat the oven to 190°C (375°F/Gas 5).

Put the tin in the oven and bake for about 25 minutes, or until the top is firm and crusty and the loaf sounds hollow when tapped. Remove from the oven, knock the loaf out of the tin and cool on a rack in a fly-free zone.

This is best eaten sliced, warm and spread with butter, but you can keep the loaf for a few days in an airtight container (not a plastic bag) for excellent toast.

**MAKES 1 LOAF OR ABOUT 18 SMALL ROLLS**

250 ml (9 fl oz/1 cup) tepid milk

15 g (½ oz) fresh yeast, crumbled, or 7 g (¼ oz) active dry yeast

1 teaspoon honey

450 g (1 lb) bread (strong) flour

½ teaspoon salt

1 egg, lightly beaten

40 g (1½ oz) butter, melted

# BOBBA'S BABKA

I remember this exaggerated puffed-up bread so well from the Jewish bakeries in South Africa and the homes of many friends. This is a recipe from my friend Lisa's gran (Bobba is Yiddish for grandma). The cinnamon just streaks through the babka and it's great alone, slightly warm, or spread with a little extra butter and jam. You can freeze the cooked bread and pull it out to thaw a couple of hours before serving.

Mix together the flour, salt and sugar in a large bowl. Crumble the yeast into a smaller bowl, add the milk and oil and mix through. Leave for 10 minutes or so to begin activating, then pour the yeast mixture into the flour mixture, scraping out the bowl well. Using an electric mixer with a dough hook, mix until well combined. Alternatively, mix with very well-floured hands.

Add the eggs and mix a little longer to combine. The dough should be thick and a little difficult to mix, even with the mixer. It will seem very sticky. Turn it out onto a floured work surface, incorporating more flour if necessary, so that it is still very sticky but not actually sticking to your hands. Work it around, kneading for about 10 minutes. Grease a large clean bowl with a little melted butter.

Put the dough in the greased bowl, turning it greased side up. Cover with plastic wrap and leave to rise in a warm place for about 1½ hours, or until it is light and doubled in size. Divide the dough in half and roll out one half on a lightly floured surface. It will still feel quite sticky. Roll it out to make a 45 x 25 cm (18 x 10 inch) rectangle that is 5 mm (¼ inch) thick.

Mix the cinnamon with the brown sugar. Spread half the butter over the rolled out dough and scatter half of the cinnamon sugar over the surface.

continues on next page …

MAKES 1 LOAF

625 g (1 lb 6 oz) cake flour or plain (all-purpose) flour

1 teaspoon salt

80 g (2¾ oz) caster (superfine) sugar

25 g (1 oz) fresh yeast, crumbled, or 15 g (½ oz) dried yeast

250 ml (9 fl oz/1 cup) tepid milk

60 ml (2¼ fl oz/¼ cup) vegetable oil

2 large eggs, lightly beaten

### CINNAMON FILLING
1 tablespoon ground cinnamon

100 g (3½ oz) dark brown sugar

60 g (2 oz) butter, softened

1 egg yolk

2 teaspoons milk

30 g (1 oz) brown sugar, to sprinkle

Roll up the dough into a long sausage along its longest edge. Set aside and do the same with the other half of the dough. Braid the two dough ropes together, pressing hard to seal the edges together. Twist the dough braid to tighten the loaf.

Put into a greased 30 cm (12 inch) loaf (bar) tin. Cover with plastic wrap and leave in a warm place for another hour or so, until it puffs up again. Preheat the oven to 180°C (350°F/Gas 4). Mix the egg yolk with the milk and brush over the top of the babka, then sprinkle with brown sugar. Put the tin in the bottom third of the oven with no shelves above it and bake for between 30–40 minutes. It will have risen more and be beautifully golden. A skewer inserted should come out clean and not have any dough sticking to it. If the ends look too brown but the dough doesn't seem cooked, cover the ends with a bit of foil and cook for a little longer. Cool for a few minutes before turning out onto a wire rack.

This is a dream served just slightly warm but it is a little more difficult to cut. It will keep for 24 hours, or toast it lightly and spread with a little butter or even a citrus curd.

# COLOURED FRUIT SALAD

I love serving bowls of colour. You could use all green fruits: say, kiwi, melon, green apples with some berries for contrast. Or golden mangoes, pineapples and oranges with a handful of strawberries thrown in.

Figs are also lovely in here — you can add anything you like as long as you use beautiful juicy sweet fruit that smells gorgeous and is the freshest of the fresh. This is also nice after a meal, with a scoop of ice cream.

**SERVES 5**

Cut up the watermelon into nice-sized chunky slithers and remove the seeds. Put in a bowl with the cherries, strawberries and peaches. Halve the pomegranate and squeeze the juice from one half into the bowl. Carefully pick out the seeds from the other half, making sure there is no white pith attached, and add to the bowl. Add the orange juice and sugar and mix together gently but thoroughly.

700 g (1 lb 9 oz) watermelon

200 g (7 oz) cherries, stoned

200 g (7 oz) small strawberries, hulled

2 smooth-skinned peaches or nectarines, stones removed, flesh sliced

1 pomegranate

juice of 1 orange

2 tablespoons caster (superfine) sugar

# HALF-MOON ROLLS

My kids love these for breakfast with butter and jam. You can freeze them easily and take out a couple as you need them. For people who have never made their own bread and think it sounds daunting, these are so much easier to make than you would think. You can even freeze the dough once it's been shaped … that way it has its second rising as it thaws.

Put the milk, water, yeast and honey in a small bowl and stir until the honey melts. Leave it for about 10 minutes, or until it begins to froth a bit.

Put the flour and salt into a larger bowl. Add the yeast mixture and melted butter and mix through well. Knead for 10 minutes or so until you have a soft elastic ball. Only add extra flour if the dough is so sticky that it is unkneadable. Cover the bowl with a cloth and leave it to rise in a warm draught-free place for 1½–2 hours, or until it has puffed up well. Punch down the dough to flatten it, and roughly divide it in half.

On a lightly floured work surface, roll or stretch each piece of dough into a circle like a pizza base, about 35 cm (14 inches) in diameter and 3 mm (⅛ inch) thick. If the dough is hard to stretch, leave it for 5 minutes to relax before rolling it out. Cut each circle into eight wedges like you would cut a pizza. Working with one wedge at a time, stretch out the two outside corners a little, then roll up the dough tightly from the outside and finishing at the point of the triangle. With this point to the top, curve the roll slightly into a crescent shape.

Line two baking trays with baking paper and arrange 8 rolls on each. Cover with a cloth and leave to rise in the warm place for 30–45 minutes. Brush with the egg and scatter the seeds over the top.

Preheat the oven to 180°C (350°F/Gas 4). Bake one tray at a time for about 15 minutes, or until the rolls are lightly golden and the bottoms sound hollow when tapped. Serve warm or at room temperature with your favourite filling.

**MAKES 16**

100 ml (3½ fl oz) tepid milk

100 ml (3½ fl oz) tepid water

15 g (½ oz) fresh yeast, crumbled, or 7 g (¼ oz) active dry yeast

1 teaspoon honey

400 g (14 oz) cake flour or plain (all-purpose) flour

½ teaspoon salt

40 g (1½ oz) butter, melted

**TO GLAZE**

1 egg, lightly beaten with a little milk

poppy seeds

sesame seeds

# SESAME SEED RINGS

I adore these for breakfast or with a meal. They are lovely bread rings that are sold by vendors on the streets in Greece. They sometimes differ in size, but generally are round, a bit flattened and slightly irregular in shape. The nice thing is that when you get them in a packet, many sesame seeds fall to the bottom, then you can pour them out and eat them off your hand.

Crumble the fresh yeast or sprinkle the dried into a bowl. Add the sugar, water and a handful of flour. Whisk to smooth any lumps. Leave until it starts to activate and bubble, about 10 minutes. Add the rest of the flour, the salt and oil and mix with a wooden spoon until a loose dough forms. Knead on a lightly floured surface for 7–8 minutes or until the dough is smooth and spongy. Wipe out the bowl with an oiled paper towel and put the dough in. Cover with plastic wrap then a tea towel and leave in a warm spot for about 2 hours until puffed and doubled in size.

Preheat the oven to 200°C (400°F/Gas 6) and line two baking trays with baking paper. For the flour paste, mix the flour and water in a bowl until smooth. Knead the dough briefly then divide it into 12 equal parts. Roll, stretch and coax each piece into a thin rope about 40 cm (16 inches) long. Make the first six and while baking, prepare the next batch. Brush each rope lightly with the paste, and sprinkle sesame seeds all over, then roll through the seeds that have dropped on your work surface so that they're covered all over. Turn each rope on itself forming a ring, pressing the ends together to seal. Place on a tray and bake for 20 minutes or until golden. Sesame seeds that have fallen onto the trays can be used elsewhere.

**MAKES 12**

25 g (1 oz) fresh yeast, or 14 g (½ oz/1 tablespoon) dried yeast
pinch of sugar
300 ml (10½ fl oz) lukewarm water
600 g (1 lb 5 oz) bread (strong) flour
1 teaspoon salt
4 tablespoons olive oil
about 150 g (5½ oz) sesame seeds

**FLOUR PASTE**
3 teaspoons bread (strong) flour
3 tablespoons water

# JAM SHORTBREAD

This is so simple and so good. I love it with any jam that's not too sweet but I usually use strawberry, raspberry or plum (it's very special with fig jam, too). It's my children's favourite kind of thing — a bit like those biscuits sandwiched together with raspberry jam that shows through the round window in front. You can use more jam if you like a lot.

Preheat the oven to 170°C (325°F/Gas 3). Have a 40 x 30 cm (16 x 12 inch) baking tray ready — you can line it if you like, to help you lift out the shortbread when it's cooked, but it's not absolutely necessary.

Put the butter and sugar in a good-sized bowl and work them together by hand or with a wooden spoon until combined. Add the flour and baking powder and work them in. Add the egg and vanilla and knead them in until it is all compact and smooth. Cover with plastic wrap and leave in the fridge for at least half an hour until the dough is firm enough to roll out.

Divide the dough in half. Roll out one half on a lightly floured surface so that it will fit into your tray. It should be 2–3 mm thick (about ⅛ inch). Fit it into your baking tray, making sure that it is a fairly even thickness all over. Spread the jam over the top, as if you were spreading it over a slice of toast. Roll out the other half of the dough and fit it as exactly as possible over the bottom one. If it is difficult to lift, roll it loosely over your rolling pin and carry it that way. It isn't essential that all your edges are exact; you can break off a bit from here and patchwork it in there. It will taste the same.

Bake for about 15 minutes, or until the shortbread is golden in places. The edges will start to turn golden brown first, followed by the top. Remove from the oven and cool for 5 minutes in the tray. Lift out of the tray, using the baking paper.

Cut into shapes with a cookie cutter, or just into squares or diamonds. Or you can leave it in one piece and keep cutting chunks out of it as you go past. It will keep in a biscuit tin for five or six days.

MAKES 12–15 PIECES, DEPENDING ON THE SIZE YOU CUT THEM

100 g (3½ oz) butter, softened
100 g (3½ oz) caster (superfine) sugar
200 g (7 oz) plain (all-purpose) flour
½ teaspoon baking powder
1 egg, lightly beaten
a few drops of vanilla extract
about 200 g (7 oz) of your favourite jam

# WHITE LOAF WITH HONEY, BUTTER & PECANS

I use a homemade white loaf to make this. If you prefer, you can use an unsliced bought one — white sourdough is good. My friend Sue taught me how to make this. I think it's fantastic — especially for a picnic. But my favourite is for breakfast.

Preheat the oven to 180°C (350°F/Gas 4) and line a baking tray with baking paper. Remove the crusts from the bread and cut it in half horizontally to give two layers (if your loaf is extra high, you can make three layers). Put the pieces on the tray.

Mix the butter, honey, sugar and pecans to get a gooey mixture. Pour and spread over the tops of the two bread halves. Bake for about 30 minutes, until the bread is crusty and golden on top. (Don't burn it or the nuts will be bitter — so take it out sooner if you see that it's ready.) Let it cool a dash, then cut into thick fingers. It will crisp up and become crunchier.

**MAKES ABOUT 16 FINGERS**

1 loaf white bread, unsliced
80 g (2¾ oz) butter, melted
100 g (3½ oz) runny honey
20 g (¾ oz) light brown sugar
50 g (1¾ oz) pecans, chopped

# GREEK YOGHURT WITH HONEY, CINNAMON, PECANS & POMEGRANATES

This is a quick 'healthy' snack that you can literally produce in one minute if you have all the ingredients. The Greek yoghurt is important — its thick and creamy nature allows the honey, nuts and cinnamon to sit on it like a crown. The pomegranate seeds dress it up well and any from the rest of the pomegranate can be served up later to nibble on with a glass of prosecco or saved for filling little tartlets.

Pick all the seeds out of the pomegranate, making sure there is no white pith still attached. In a small dry frying pan, lightly toast the pecans just enough to bring out their flavour and crisp them up (take care not to overdo them or they'll be bitter and taste burnt). Leave them to cool.

Spoon the yoghurt into bowls, scatter a small fistful of nuts over the top, drizzle with honey and finish with a small scattering of pomegranate seeds and cinnamon. Best served immediately.

**SERVES 2**

seeds from ¼ pomegranate

about 25 g (1 oz) pecans, broken into big chunks

300 g (10½ oz) Greek-style natural yoghurt

4 teaspoons thick runny honey

ground cinnamon

# CHOCOLATE LOAF

This is a wonderful addition to your breakfast table. Despite its looks, it is definitely a bread and is quite a surprise, so you might need to prepare people who are expecting it to be a cake. It is beautiful plain, or toasted with butter or homemade mandarin or strawberry jam.

Crumble the yeast into a large bowl and add the sugar. Gently heat the milk in a small saucepan until it feels just a bit hotter than your finger, then add it to the yeast. Stir through and leave for 10 minutes or so, until the surface starts to turn spongy. Add the flour, cocoa powder, butter and a pinch of salt and mix in well. Knead with your hands for about 6 minutes until the dough is smooth and elastic with no lumps. If your dough is very soft, leave it in the bowl and just punch it around and squeeze it with one hand, holding the bowl with the other. Cover the bowl with a heavy tea towel and leave it in a warm and draught-free place for 1½–2 hours until it has puffed right up. Butter and flour a 30 x 11 cm (12 x 4¼ inch) loaf (bar) tin.

Knock the dough down to flatten it and shape it to the size of the tin. Drop it in, cover the tin with the tea towel and leave it again in a warm place for anywhere between 30 minutes and an hour, until the dough has puffed up over the rim of the tin. While the dough is rising, preheat the oven to 180°C (350°F/Gas 4).

Remove the tea towel and bake the loaf for about 25 minutes, or until the top is firm and the bread sounds hollow when tapped on the bottom. Tip out onto a rack to cool. Once it has cooled down completely, this loaf can be frozen (even just a chunk of it) in a plastic bag and saved for another moment in time.

**MAKES 1 LOAF**

15 g (½ oz) fresh yeast

40 g (1½ oz) caster (superfine) sugar

310 ml (10¾ fl oz/1¼ cups) milk

400 g (14 oz) bread (strong) flour or plain (all-purpose) flour

40 g (1½ oz) unsweetened cocoa powder

40 g (1½ oz) butter, melted

# 2

~ SMALL BITES ~

# BAKED STUFFED VINE LEAVES

This wonderful way of preparing *dolmades* comes from my friend Artemis's mum, Christina. It is a more unusual vegetarian version than you may find readily available in Greece and completely delicious. It is very easy to double the quantity, and they keep well for the next day, so it's worth making a good amount. Christina makes at least seventy at a time — it can be fun to sit at a table and work, hopefully with someone helping you.

MAKES 35–40

If using bought leaves, put them in a bowl of water to soak for a few minutes. Drain, pat dry with paper towels then stack in piles for later. Using the large holes of a grater, grate the onion, mushrooms, carrot, zucchini and tomatoes, keeping them separate for now. Heat 3 tablespoons of oil in a wide pot and sauté the onion until golden. Add the mushrooms, carrot and zucchini and sauté for 10 minutes or so. Stir in the rice, grated tomato, then the parsley, mint and lemon juice and season with salt and black pepper. Simmer for 5 minutes. Remove from the heat and stir in the *kefalotiri*.

Preheat the oven to 180°C (350°F/Gas 4). Spread a few whole vine leaves at a time on your work surface, shiny side down. Spoon a heaped tablespoon of filling onto each leaf and roll up neatly and snugly, tucking in the sides after the first roll and continuing to roll. Line them up in a baking dish. They should just fit but if not, stack the last few on top. Add 250 ml (9 fl oz/1 cup) of water and drizzle over the remaining oil. Sprinkle with salt and pepper. Rock the dish two or three times to distribute the liquid. Cover with foil. Bake for 1 hour then uncover and bake for 10 minutes or so.

- 35–40 good vine leaves, plus a few torn ones
- 1 red onion, peeled
- 250 g (9 oz) mushrooms, such as Swiss brown or field
- 1 carrot, peeled
- 200 g (7 oz) zucchini (courgettes)
- 3 large tomatoes
- 1 Greek coffee cup (about 4 tablespoons) olive oil
- 100 g (3½ oz) medium-grain rice
- 3 tablespoons chopped flat-leaf parsley
- ½ tablespoon dried mint
- juice of 1 lemon
- 3 tablespoons grated *kefalotiri* or parmesan cheese

# TUNA OR SARDINE PÂTÉ

Tuna or sardine pâté comes before every meal in Portugal, it seems. It is on the table as soon as you sit down, in tiny pre-packed butter-like parcels, to be spread over some lovely bread. You can add whatever flavourings you might like here … some more lemon, chopped parsley or any other herb. Make sure the butter and fish are well puréed so there are no lumps. Depending on the butter and anchovies you use, you might not need any extra salt.

MAKES ABOUT 200 G (7 OZ/1 CUP)

### TUNA

Use a hand-held blender or pulse the butter, tuna and anchovies in a food processor to blend. Sprinkle in the lemon juice, piri piri, some pepper, salt if needed, and blend again. Cover and refrigerate for up to a few days if you are not serving immediately (but take it out of the fridge well before you serve, so that it's not rock hard). This is lovely spread on warm toast.

### SARDINE

Use a hand-held blender or pulse the butter, tomato paste and sardines in a food processor to blend well. Sprinkle in the whisky, piri piri, pepper and a little salt, if you like, and blend until smooth. Fold in the parsley.

Cover and refrigerate for up to a few days if you are not serving immediately (but take it out of the fridge well before you do serve, so that it's not rock hard).

### TUNA

100 g (3½ oz) unsalted butter

100 g (3½ oz) tinned best-quality tuna in oil, drained

2 anchovies packed in oil, drained

a splash of lemon juice

a pinch of ground piri piri

### SARDINE

100 g (3½ oz) unsalted butter

1 teaspoon tomato paste (concentrated purée)

120 g (4¼ oz) tinned Portuguese sardines in oil, drained

a splash of whisky

a pinch of ground piri piri

some chopped flat-leaf parsley, if you like

# PRAWN PASTRIES

This might seem a touch long and fiddly, but you could break up the workload: make the prawn filling and pastry in the morning, keep it in the fridge, bring back to room temperature, then roll and refrigerate and fry the pastries before dinner, say. These are really wonderful as an appetiser before a seafood meal, or as a simple lunch with a big green salad. You could also add a grating or two of fresh nutmeg in place of the paprika and some coriander or other herbs instead of the parsley.

MAKES ABOUT 20

To make the pastry, put the milk, salt, butter and 150 ml (5 fl oz) of water in a smallish heavy-based saucepan and bring to the boil. Just as it starts to come to the boil, take the pan off the heat and pour in the flour all in one go. Stir with a wooden spoon, then put it back on the heat, mixing until it all comes together in a ball. Leave to cool.

Make the filling. Simmer the prawns and bay leaf in the milk mixed with 125 ml (4 fl oz/½ cup) of water for 5 minutes or so until just cooked but still tender. Remove from the heat and drain, keeping the liquid. Peel the prawns, discarding the shells, and roughly chop.

Heat the butter in a small non-stick frying pan and sauté the shallot. When it starts to turn golden, add the celery and sauté until that too is golden, then add the parsley, piri piri, paprika and garlic. When you start to smell the garlic, add the tomato paste. Cook for a moment, then stir in the flour and finally add all the prawn cooking liquid. Boil up, then reduce the heat and simmer for 5 minutes or so until thickened. Remove from the heat, stir in the prawns, lemon zest and juice and season with salt and pepper. Leave to cool slightly.

continues on next page …

**PASTRY**
150 ml (5 fl oz) milk
½ teaspoon salt
50 g (1¾ oz) butter
250 g (9 oz) plain (all-purpose) flour

**FILLING**
180 g (6½ oz) raw prawns (shrimp) with shells but no heads
1 bay leaf
125 ml (4 fl oz/½ cup) milk
50 g (1¾ oz) butter

continues on next page …

Lightly dust your work surface with flour. Pat your hands in flour and pat the top of the pastry too. Roll out to about 2 mm (1/16 inch) thick (you might find it easier to roll the pastry in two lots). Cut out 10 cm (4 inch) circles with a pastry cutter and dollop a heaped teaspoon of filling in the middle of each one. Dip your finger in water and run it along the edge of the pastry. Turn over and push down on the edge firmly to seal. Keep rolling out the scraps of pastry — you should get about 20 parcels.

Whip the egg with some salt and pepper in a flattish bowl. Put the breadcrumbs onto a plate. Pour enough oil into a large frying pan to come about halfway up the pastries when they're frying, and line a plate with paper towel ready for draining them.

Dip the well-sealed pastries in the egg, turning to coat both sides. Pat in breadcrumbs on both sides while your oil is heating (not too hot, or they'll burn before they cook through), then put the pastries in the pan — as many as will fit in a single layer. Fry until the undersides are beautifully golden, then turn them over with tongs or an egg slice, taking care not to pierce them. Fry until golden and crisp, then drain on paper towel while you fry the rest. Eat warm with lemon juice and salt.

The pastries can also be frozen before dipping in egg and breadcrumbs. Freeze them on a tray, crack them off and put them into a container flash frozen.

**Note:** Fresh breadcrumbs are best for coating. Just pulse two- or three-day-old country-style bread in a food processor. You can keep these in the freezer and top them up whenever you have leftover bread.

1 shallot, finely chopped

1 small celery stalk, finely chopped

2 tablespoons chopped flat-leaf parsley

a good pinch of ground piri piri

1/4 teaspoon sweet paprika

1 garlic clove, chopped

2 teaspoons tomato paste (concentrated purée)

2 tablespoons plain (all-purpose) flour

grated zest and juice from 1/2 a small lemon

1 large egg, lightly beaten

about 3 cupfuls of breadcrumbs, to coat (see note)

olive oil, for frying

lemon wedges, to serve

# KOUPES

These are a wonderful Middle Eastern speciality. It is good to have a couple of friends helping, as they can be a little tricky, but once you have tasted *koupes* you will want to know how to make your own. They are shaped like long dumplings or elongated eggs with slightly pointed ends. The outer shell is made with burghul wheat and filled with a mixture of fried mince (ground) meat, parsley, cinnamon and pine nuts, then deep-fried. Women who have been making these for a lifetime casually churn out these burghul shells as though they were knitting or doing something quite natural. If you use minced lamb in the shells as well as the burghul, you will find them a lot easier to shape, so I've included both methods.

If you are feeling brave, or have made these before, you can make the shells from just burghul wheat. Put 500 g (1 lb 2 oz) of burghul in a bowl, season with salt and cover with 625 ml (21½ fl oz/2½ cups) of just-boiled water. Mix through and, once the wheat has cooled a little, cover the bowl and leave for about 3 hours while you make the filling.

To make the shells by the easier method, put the lamb mince in a food processor and blend to a paste. Transfer to a bowl. Blend the onions to a paste as well, add to the mince and season well with salt and pepper. Mix well and set aside. Rinse the burghul wheat in a sieve under cold running water. Drain well and squeeze out any excess water. Blend in a food processor. Add the mince mixture and blend again. Set aside while you make the filling.

To make the filling, heat the olive oil in a non-stick pan and sauté the onion, stirring, until softened and lightly golden. Add the mince and continue to sauté until all the moisture from the meat has evaporated and it is golden and completely cooked. Break up any clusters with a wooden spoon. Season with salt and pepper and add the cinnamon, stirring constantly to prevent the meat from sticking. Add the pine nuts and cook for another minute or two. Stir in the parsley, then remove from the heat to cool.

continues on next page …

MAKES 25 KOUPES

## SHELLS
115 g (4 oz/⅔ cup) fine burghul (bulgar) wheat or 500 g (1 lb 2 oz) fine burghul (and no lamb, see method)

500 g (1 lb 2 oz) lean minced (ground) lamb

2 red onions, chopped

## FILLING
1 tablespoon olive oil

1 white onion, finely chopped

300 g (10½ oz) minced (ground) pork and beef

½ teaspoon ground cinnamon

30 g (1 oz) pine nuts

15 g (½ oz/½ cup) chopped flat-leaf parsley

oil, for deep-frying

lemons, to serve

Now you are ready to make the shells. Have a small bowl of water ready. If you are using the shell mixture with just burghul, start kneading the burghul wheat in the bowl and then turn it out onto the work surface and knead it as you would a dough (although it will be much harder). It should start to feel softer after a while and then you can break off a chunk about the size of an egg and make it into a ball. If you are using the shell mixture with meat in it, take a ball of the shell mixture about the size of an egg (keep the rest of the mixture covered with a damp cloth to prevent it drying out).

Hold the ball in the cup of your left hand (if you are right-handed). Using your right thumb, flatten the ball so that it takes the shape of your palm, turning upwards like a blanket, and is as thin as you can make it. Add a teaspoonful of the filling mixture and fold the sides of the 'blanket' over the filling. Now you need to seal the top, so, if there is enough shell then do so by dipping your hands lightly in water and using it like glue if you find it helps. Or add more shell mixture, pressing it to make uniform, and then cup your hands together, cradling the shell tightly to make it smooth and compact. Put this on a tray while you make the rest.

Fill a saucepan or deep-fryer with enough oil that it will cover the *koupes* and heat it for deep-frying. Add the *koupes* a few at a time and deep-fry for 2–3 minutes until dark golden and crisp. Drain on paper towel to absorb the excess oil and then serve drizzled with lemon juice and an extra sprinkling of salt. These are also good served at room temperature.

# MEAT CARPACCIO

I like to serve this with artichoke and a lemon oil. You could also serve it with rocket (arugula), or thin slices of endive, fennel or celeriac. A couple of blobs of a creamy blue cheese here and there also work well. Serve this as an *antipasto* for two or a *secondo* for one. It is lovely as a summer lunch with a green salad on the side and some bread, and then it can take something slightly richer for dessert.

Use well-trimmed and tender flavoursome lean beef such as girello or shell steak (use strip loin or porterhouse), tenderloin (mid loin) or beef fillet also work well. The diameter of the meat is not important; just add more slices to the plate to cover it, overlapping slightly if necessary. Ask the butcher to trim the meat for you. You may even be able to convince him to slice it, but only if you plan to serve it within an hour or two. If you slice the meat yourself, cut it very cold from the fridge to get the thinnest possible slices. It is important the meat is thin thin and soft soft. Add some coarse pounded salt in too for the texture — table salt with a small amount of bashed coarse salt added.

Prepare your artichoke first. Trim away the outer leaves and cut a slice off the top. Halve the artichoke and remove the hairy choke if it has one, then cut each half into fine slices 1–2 mm (1/16 inch) thick. (If you're not serving immediately, keep them covered with cold water and a little lemon juice to prevent them turning black.)

If necessary, put the beef slices between two sheets of plastic wrap and pound with a meat mallet until very thin. Arrange them flat on a large plate, slightly overlapping is fine. Scatter the artichoke slices over the top. Drizzle with lemon juice, sprinkle with the salt and drizzle with oil. Now scatter the cheese on top and a good grind of black pepper. Serve with bread and perhaps the bottle of olive oil, salt and black pepper on the side in case you need extra.

**SERVES 2**

1 beautiful artichoke suitable for eating raw

125 g (4½ oz) very thinly sliced beef

juice of ½ a lemon

table and coarse pounded salt, to taste

2 tablespoons extra virgin olive oil

about 20 g (¾ oz) shaved parmesan cheese

bread, to serve

# FISH CARPACCIO

You can use any type of the freshest seafood for this dish, such as
scampi (langoustines), razor clams, prawns (shrimp) and the like,
and an oyster or two could be added. I have also made this with
smoked swordfish, which was really good. There is no real need
to marinate the fish at all — once the dressing has been added, it
will be very tasty, but I normally marinate for anywhere between
ten minutes and one hour. One of the most important requirements
is to slice the fish most finely. If you're not confident of your
knife skills, ask your fishmonger to slice the fish about 2 mm
(1/16 inch) thick.

SERVES 4

You will need two large plates with rims. Rub each plate with the garlic
clove, covering as much of the plate as you can. Wrap the peppercorns in
a thick piece of paper towel and gently press down with your palms to lightly
crush them — it is nice if many remain whole, just lightly pressed
to release their flavour.

Lay the fish slices out flat, with the tuna on one plate and swordfish on the
other. If necessary, overlap the slices. Dribble half the olive oil and lemon
juice over each plate and scatter half the peppercorns onto each. Season with
a pinch of dried ground chilli, if you like, and some salt and pepper. Leave
at room temperature for 10 minutes or so. Once the fish starts to change
colour slightly it's ready to serve. (It could also stay in the fridge, covered,
for an hour.)

Before serving, scatter parsley over one plate and thyme over the other
(I like parsley for the swordfish and thyme for the tuna). Taste the fish and
if necessary add a little more salt or other seasoning.

1 garlic clove, peeled and halved

2 good teaspoons dried pink
peppercorns

140 g (5 oz) thick tuna fillet, very,
very thinly sliced

140 g (5 oz) thick swordfish fillet,
very, very thinly sliced

3–4 tablespoons best extra virgin
olive oil

juice of 2 small lemons

a pinch of dried ground chilli, if you
like

1 scant tablespoon chopped flat-leaf
parsley

leaves of 1 fresh thyme sprig

# TINY SAVOURY TARTLETS

I always make these for children's birthdays. They are just the right size to pop into a child's mouth. Adults love them, too, and you can be as modern as you like with your fillings. The number of pastry shells you get will depend on the size of your cases. Mine are tiny individual ones, while some are punched into a tray of twelve or twenty-four.

For the pastry, put the butter and flour in a bowl with the salt and crumble with your fingers until it is like coarse sand. Add 3 tablespoons of cold water and the oil and work into a loose dough. Knead quickly but gently until smooth, then flatten, cover with plastic wrap and refrigerate for about an hour.

Preheat the oven to 180°C (350°F/Gas 4) and have ready 45 tiny tart cases that are 4.5 cm (1¾ inches) across the top and no more than 2 cm (¾ inch) deep. They don't need to be greased (there is enough butter in the dough).

Break off small balls of pastry about the size of cherry tomatoes and flatten into the cases with your thumb and forefinger, pressing to a couple of millimetres thick. (If your cases are shallow you could roll out the pastry first, then press into the cases and trim the excess pastry away.) Bake for about 20 minutes, or until golden, and then cool a bit in the cases before gently removing. Leave to cool completely before filling.

These can be made the day before and kept in an airtight container overnight.

The tartlets are best with something creamy to balance the pastry. Any soft cheese like mozzarella works well and sometimes I like to use 250 g (9 oz/1 cup) smooth ricotta mixed with 25 g (1 oz) grated parmesan, 1 scant tablespoon olive oil, the juice of half a lemon and a little fresh thyme. I fill all the cases with this, then top with any of the following:

~ roasted tomatoes, basil oil, parmesan flakes;

~ smoked salmon, dill sprigs, a drizzle of lemon juice;

~ *bresaola* or prosciutto, torn basil leaves, parmesan flakes.

**MAKES ABOUT 40 TARTLET CASES**

**PASTRY**
125 g (4½ oz) butter, cut into cubes
250 g (9 oz) plain (all-purpose) flour
½ teaspoon salt
½ tablespoon olive oil

**FILLING IDEAS**
~ soft-boiled eggs mashed with olive oil and chopped flat-leaf parsley;
~ avocado mashed with lemon juice and sweet paprika;
~ 320 g (11¼ oz) tinned tuna in oil mashed with 3 soft-boiled eggs, a chopped spring onion (scallion), 1 tablespoon chopped flat-leaf parsley, 2 tablespoons mayonnaise, the juice of 1 lemon, a pinch of sweet paprika and 2 tablespoons light olive oil.

# PRAWNS WITH PIRI PIRI WHISKY & LEMON

Tavira is a wonderfully sleepy, ancient town in Portugal's south.
I ate this one night in a small restaurant there and it was so lovely
that I asked the lady how she made it. This makes a perfect starter
before a main course of grilled fish.

SERVES 3–4

Remove the heads from the prawns but leave the shells on the bodies. Make a shallow cut down the back of each one so they take in the flavour of the sauce and devein them. Rinse and pat dry.

Heat the oil and half the butter in a large non-stick saucepan until very hot and sizzling. Throw in the prawns and bay leaves gradually, trying not to lose the heat, so the prawns get crusty and golden. Toss the pan and season with coarse salt and pepper. When the prawns are nicely golden on both sides, add the garlic, parsley, as much piri piri as you like, the paprika and the last of the butter.

Toss until you can smell the garlic, then add the whisky. When it's been absorbed, add the lemon juice and toss it all together. Let it bubble up for a moment, check the seasoning, then use a slotted spoon to lift the prawns onto a plate.

Add about 4 tablespoons of water to the pan and let it bubble up to thicken the sauce. Remove from the heat, return the prawns to the pan and toss through the sauce. Serve with some bread for the sauce and a lemon wedge or two.

400 g (14 oz) raw prawns (shrimp)

1 tablespoon olive oil

50 g (1¾ oz) butter

2 small bay leaves

2 garlic cloves, chopped

1 tablespoon chopped flat-leaf parsley

ground piri piri (or other chilli powder)

½ teaspoon sweet paprika

3–4 tablespoons whisky

juice of 1 small lemon

extra lemons, to serve

# SPINACH & TRUFFLE PIES

I love individual pastries like these, which are served in many countries. These ones take an Italian direction. You should be able to find a mushroom *'crema'* perfumed with truffle in an Italian delicatessen. The one I use is a purée of porcini and other wild mushrooms.

MAKES 16

To make the pastry, sift the flour and a pinch of salt into a bowl. Add the butter and stir through to coat it with flour. Add enough of the iced water to make the dough come together. Gather into a ball and transfer to a floured work surface. Flour your hands and form the dough into a block. Roll this out to make a rectangle about 1 cm (½ inch) thick with the short side closest to you. Fold up the bottom third of the rectangle and fold down the top third. Seal the edges lightly with a rolling pin. Turn the dough through 90 degrees and roll it out again into a rectangle that is about 5 mm (¼ inch) thick. Fold as before, turn the dough and roll out again. Do this once more, then put the dough in a plastic bag and leave in the fridge for 30 minutes.

Blanch the spinach in boiling salted water for about 5 minutes, or until it is soft, then drain well and squeeze out the excess water. Pass half the spinach through a mincer with the mozzarella so that it is very finely chopped. Chop up the remaining spinach by hand to keep some texture in the filling (or chop it all by hand if you don't have a mincer). Mix in the mushroom 'crema', olive oil and truffle oil and season with salt and pepper.

Preheat the oven to 200°C (400°F/Gas 6). Line a baking tray with baking paper. Roll out the pastry to make a square just larger than 40 cm (16 inches). Trim away the edges to make a neat square. Now cut lengthways and breadthways to make sixteen squares of 10 cm (4 inches) each.

Dollop a tablespoon of the spinach mixture in the centre of each square, then fold over to form a triangle, pressing the edges down to seal. Arrange the pies on the baking tray and brush the tops with beaten egg. Bake for 10–15 minutes or until they are golden and the undersides are also firm and golden. Leave them to cool a little, just so you don't burn your mouth.

- 225 g (8 oz) plain (all-purpose) flour
- 225 g (8 oz) chilled butter, diced
- 4–5 tablespoons iced water
- 375 g (13 oz) English spinach leaves
- 100 g (3½ oz) mozzarella (drained weight)
- 1 tablespoon *crema di funghi al tartufo* (cream of mushrooms with truffle)
- 1 tablespoon olive oil
- 1 teaspoon truffle oil
- 1 egg, beaten, for brushing

# BAKED SCALLOPS

This makes abundant saucy topping for six scallops, or even more if yours are on the smaller side. It's easy enough to double the sauce recipe if you want to use more scallops. You can buy scallops already prepared on the half shell.

Preheat the oven to very hot: 220°C (425°F/Gas 7). Mix the garlic, lemon, parsley and olive oil together and drizzle generously over the scallops. Scatter with breadcrumbs (a three-finger pinch per scallop) and salt and pepper and put a small blob of butter on top of each.

Put the scallops on a baking tray or in an oven dish lined with foil (just to save on cleaning) and roast for about 10–15 minutes until tender and with crusty golden tops and bubbling juice. Serve with bread.

**SERVES 2–3**

1 large garlic clove, finely chopped

2–3 tablespoons lemon juice

1½ tablespoons finely chopped flat-leaf parsley

2 tablespoons olive oil

6 scallops with coral, on the half shell

dry breadcrumbs

2 teaspoons butter

# FRIED MOZZARELLA TOASTS

These delicious little sandwiches make great snacks and are great for keeping hunger at bay. Use a small pan that will fit two sandwiches at a time so you don't need too much oil. These are also good without the béchamel but then they are less creamy and soft inside. You can make the béchamel ahead of time if you like — it's fine to use cold.

MAKES 4

To make the béchamel, melt the butter in a small heavy-based saucepan. Whisk the flour into the butter and cook for a few minutes, stirring. Reduce the heat to low, then add half the warm milk, whisking well. Add the rest of the milk, a grating of nutmeg and some salt. Keep whisking until the sauce is smooth and thick, then remove the pan from the heat, cover and set aside to firm up a bit. Even completely cooled, this is fine to use.

To make the dipping mixture, beat together the eggs, milk and salt in a flat bowl.

For the mozzarella and ham sandwiches, spread 1 scant teaspoon of béchamel over all 4 slices of bread, right to the edge. Lay a piece of ham and 2 or 3 slices of mozzarella onto 2 pieces of the bread so that the topping comes right to the edge. Top with the other pieces of bread to make two sandwiches and press together firmly to seal well. Heat the oil in a pan — not too hot. Pat the sandwiches in flour, then dip in the dipping mixture to coat well. Shake them out of the mixture and let them drain off a bit, then press in the breadcrumbs to coat all over. Fry in the hot oil, turning when golden and crisp on the bottom to cook the other side, then transfer to a plate lined with paper towel. Eat warm, taking care not to burn your mouth on the hot filling.

Variation: For mozzarella and anchovy sandwiches, spread 1 scant teaspoon of béchamel over all 4 slices of bread. Dab a little anchovy paste onto each piece here and there (about ¼ teaspoon onto each). Lay 2 or 3 slices of mozzarella onto 2 pieces of bread to come right to the edge, then top with pieces of anchovy fillet. Top with the other pieces of bread to make two sandwiches and press together firmly to seal well. Dip in the flour, egg and breadcrumbs and fry as above.

**BÉCHAMEL SAUCE**
1 scant tablespoon butter
3 teaspoons plain (all-purpose) flour
125 ml (4 fl oz/½ cup) warm milk
a grating of nutmeg

**DIPPING MIXTURE**
2 eggs
1 tablespoon milk
a pinch of salt
plain (all-purpose) flour, for coating
dry breadcrumbs

**FOR 2 MOZZARELLA & HAM SANDWICHES**
4 slices of white sandwich bread, crusts removed
4–6 slices (not too thick) mozzarella cheese
1 large slice of ham, halved or 2 small pieces of ham
light olive oil, for frying

# SERGIA'S BREW

This is delicious as an appetiser but is also fantastic in summer with tuna, or served over pasta. Sergia makes and sells this in her alimentari in Venice's Calle dei Do Mori. Originally, there were twenty-seven alimentari shops in the city; now there is one: Sergia's. She's like a mix between a great grandmother owl and a film star. I first met her when I stopped in at her shop and asked where she would send me to eat lunch with locals. So she closed her shop and accompanied me to her friend Marinella's, and at 4 pm we were still drinking Valpolicella and chatting. Now, whenever I stand in Sergia's shop I am amazed by the amount of social goings-on: the milk guy who pops in to exchange chatter and news, a quick visit from one of Sergia's seven grandchildren or other relatives, or a conversation with the man who knows about all the foundations of Venice. Sergia keeps introducing everyone and at the same time carries on calmly helping customers in her gentle way. Next comes a guy whom Sergia announces might give me a good recipe for goose, and so time goes on.

Mix everything together in a large bowl — don't worry about being gentle. Keep covered in the fridge. As the oil chills and solidifies, the mixture will meld into one mass so that you won't be able to work out what it is, but once you remove it from the fridge, the oil melts. Store in the fridge, covered with the oil, for up to a week.

Serve with bread, holding back some of the oil as it may be heavy. This is also lovely with cooked penne.

**SERVES MANY**

150 g (5½ oz) drained kalamata olives in oil

100 g (3½ oz) drained pitted taggiasche olives in oil

80 g (2¾ oz) drained large green olives

80 g (2¾ oz) drained sun-dried tomatoes in oil, halved lengthways

100 g (3½ oz) caprini (smooth goat's cheese), broken into chunks

about 200 g (7 oz) buffalo mozzarella, cut into chunks

½ teaspoon dried oregano

a good pinch of dried ground chilli

about 250 ml (9 fl oz/1 cup) good olive oil

# GRATINÉED MUSSELS

This is Daniela's recipe. She is Portuguese and was born in Mozambique, and her parents now live in Lisbon. She's a wonderful cook and these, I think, are fabulous to precede any seafood meal. Before you start cooking your mussels you need to 'de-beard' them by pulling away those fiddly bits of algae that stick out. Cut them off with scissors or a knife if you can't detach them, then scrub the shells well with a wire brush to dislodge evidence of the sea. At this stage you need to discard any mussels that are open and don't close when you give them a tap.

Fresh breadcrumbs are best for sprinkling over the top: just pulse two- or three-day-old country-style bread in a food processor. You can keep these in the freezer and top them up whenever you have leftover bread.

MAKES 24

Put your cleaned mussels into a pot, add the whole garlic clove, a couple of splashes of white wine, the parsley sprigs and some salt and pepper. Turn the heat to high, cover the pot and steam for about 3 minutes, or until the mussels open (discard any that remain stubbornly closed). Leave to cool. (You don't need the liquid here, but it's nice to stir into some simmering rice to serve later.) You can steam the mussels beforehand if it's helpful, and leave to cool with the lid on.

Preheat the oven to 200°C (400°F/Gas 6). Pick the mussels out of the shells and save the shell halves — you won't use all the shells (you'll need about 24), so pick out the best clean sides without the point at which the mussel was attached, and save some extra just in case. Put the shell halves in a single layer in a dish that can go from oven to table.

Chop the mussel meat finely. Heat the olive oil in a small pan and sauté the shallot until golden. Add the chopped garlic and stir until you start to smell it. Add the mussel meat, lemon juice, chopped parsley, piri piri and some salt and pepper. Cook for just a moment once you've added the mussels, then turn off the heat when it is still a bit liquidy.

Spoon a teaspoonful of the mussel mixture into each shell so they are not too tightly packed. Sprinkle lightly with breadcrumbs and gratinée in the oven for 10 minutes, or until a bit golden but not dried out. Serve straight from the oven, or at room temperature.

about 35 largish mussels, cleaned (as above)

3 garlic cloves, peeled, 1 left whole and 2 finely chopped

2–3 tablespoons white wine

2 flat-leaf parsley sprigs

1 tablespoon olive oil

1 shallot, finely chopped

juice of ½ a lemon

2 heaped tablespoons chopped flat-leaf parsley

a good pinch of ground piri piri

breadcrumbs, for sprinkling

# FRIED CHEESE

In Greece, there is a typical pan called a *saganaki*, which is used for cooking and serving this — it's a small pan with handles on either side. You can use *kasseri*, *kefalotiri* or a softer type of Greek cheese such as *talagani*, which is my favourite for this savoury version. Serve hot with lemon on the side for squeezing over.

Pour the olive oil into a small non-stick frying pan to a depth of roughly 1 cm (½ inch).

Put the egg in one flat bowl and the flour in another. Heat up the oil. Dip the cheese slice in the egg then pat it in the flour to coat well. Put the slice into the oil and fry until golden on both sides. Splash its sides with oil to make sure that they are fried golden too. The cheese must be crisp on the outside and softened on the inside. When done, remove the cheese from the pan with tongs and drain on paper towel. Serve hot, cut up into squares and with lemon juice squeezed over the top. If serving in the same dish, remove the cheese, pour away the oil, wipe the dish with paper towel, return the cheese to the dish and squeeze some lemon over.

**SERVES 4**

light olive oil, for frying
1 egg, lightly beaten
plain (all-purpose) flour, to coat
120 g (4¼ oz), 2 cm (¾ inch) thick slice of *kasseri*-style cheese, or *talagani*
lemon quarters, to serve

# 3

## ~ SOUPS ~

# PORTUGUESE GASPACHO

Piri piri for serving is a must here. The gaspacho I had in Portugal was nice and cold and had all different sizes of vegetables — but none too big — a little oil, some oregano and a splash of vinegar. I had hoped for a port vinegar for this, so mingling the red wine vinegar with a little port lifted the gaspacho to new heights. Add more vinegar if you like; keep tasting to get the balance right for your own tastes. Serve with crusty bread, or just put some torn bread in the bowl.

SERVES 4–6

Put the onion in a small bowl, cover with cold water, scatter with a teaspoon of coarse salt and leave for an hour or so. Prepare the tomatoes by peeling off the skin with a small sharp knife. Cut them in half through the middle and hold over a fine sieve, which in turn is over a bowl to catch the juice. Remove the seeds (dropping them into the sieve), then dice the tomatoes.

Hold the cucumber upright and divide into 4 thick slices vertically. Then cut each fat slice into long batons and chop these. The very middle seedy part can be removed if you like, or left if you prefer.

Put into a big bowl (even the one that you will use for serving) and add 2 teaspoons or so of coarse salt. Mix in the chopped peppers and celery, the bay leaves and chopped tomatoes with their juice. Add 500 ml (17 fl oz/ 2 cups) of cold water and stir in the parsley and oregano. Grind some pepper over the top, cover and leave in the fridge for an hour or so.

Put the garlic clove in a small bowl with the oil, vinegar and port and leave to marinate. Take the gaspacho out of the fridge, add the oil and vinegar (discarding the garlic) and the rinsed and drained onion. Mix well, then taste for the seasonings and adjust any flavours that need it. Keep in the fridge if you won't be serving immediately. Definitely serve with several splashes of a piri piri sauce or oil.

1 small red onion, finely chopped

coarse salt

about 400 g (14 oz) very ripe tomatoes

1 cucumber, peeled

1 green pepper (capsicum), seeded and chopped

1 red pepper (capsicum), seeded and chopped

1 celery stalk with leaves, chopped

2 small fresh bay leaves

1–2 tablespoons chopped parsley

¾ teaspoon dried oregano

1 garlic clove, peeled and a bit squashed

3 tablespoons olive oil

2–3 tablespoons red wine vinegar, or more to taste

about 1 tablespoon port

piri piri sauce or oil, to serve

# POTATO & CABBAGE SOUP WITH CHOURIÇO

This *caldo verde* must be the culinary equivalent of the Portuguese flag and it could be a meal in itself with bread. A small bowlful is perfect as a first course if you've got the barbecue going for something else afterwards (the Portuguese do seem to serve up soup as their 'vegetable' and then just meat and potatoes for the main). You can use any dark cabbage — couve, cavolo nero, kale or even savoy — but trim away the thick stems, roll up the leaves into a cigar and slice very very thinly.

**SERVES 4**

Heat the oil in a wide pan and sauté the onions, stirring often because there isn't much oil, until soft and sticky. Add the garlic and potato chunks, stirring while they cook until you start to smell the garlic. Add 1.25 litres (44 fl oz/ 5 cups) of water and the bay leaves and bring to the boil. Season with a good heaped teaspoon of salt, lower the heat slightly, cover the pan and simmer for 20 minutes or so, until the potatoes are cooked but not soggy. Remove from the heat.

Meanwhile, bring a large pot of salted water to the boil, add the cabbage and simmer for 10 minutes. With a slotted spoon, remove 2 spoonfuls of potato from the pan and keep on one side. (And discard the bay leaves.) Purée the rest of the soup until completely smooth and then return to the heat. Use your slotted spoon to add the cabbage to the puréed soup, together with about a cupful of its cooking water (or however much you think it needs). Let it simmer for 5 minutes or so and then add the unpuréed potato near the end so that everything mingles. Check the seasoning, turn off the heat and cover the pan while you prepare the *chouriço*.

You need your barbecue or chargrill pan to be hot as hot. Cook the *chouriço* until it's golden and charred here and there, then cut into slices. Ladle the soup into bowls and top each with a few slices of sausage. Add a drizzle of piri piri oil or sauce for some heat, if you like.

**2 tablespoons olive oil**

**2 red onions, chopped**

**2 garlic cloves, chopped**

**700 g (1 lb 9 oz) potatoes, peeled and cut into chunks**

**2 bay leaves**

**200 g (7 oz) dark cabbage, stems removed, very thinly sliced**

**60 g (2¼ oz) *chouriço* sausage**

**piri piri oil or sauce, for drizzling**

# FISHERMAN'S SOUP

This is the type of chunky soup that a Greek fisherman would make on his boat. Often the fish are left whole, but here I have first made a broth, strained it, and then cooked fillets of fish in it to avoid bones swimming around. It is so simple. Potatoes, onions, garlic, chunks of tomato and fish.

SERVES 4

Make a broth. Put the soup fish into a stockpot and cover with 1 litre (35 fl oz/4 cups) of cold water. Add most of the bunch of parsley, but save some to coarsely chop for serving later (you'll need about 2 heaped tablespoons). Add the piece of celery, the whole garlic clove, salt and a couple of grinds of pepper. Peel the onion and cut off a piece from one side. Add this piece to the stockpot. Chop what's left of the onion and put to one side for the moment. Bring the pot to the boil. Lower the heat and simmer for about 20 minutes. Strain, discarding the bones and skin of the fish as well as the herbs and vegetables. You should have about 750 ml (26 fl oz/3 cups) of broth. Depending on the fish you've used, you may be able to salvage some flesh for another use.

Heat the oil in a large wide pot and sauté the chopped onion until softened and pale golden. Add the chopped celery and sauté until that softens too. Next add the chopped garlic and cook until you can smell it, then add the wine. Cook until the wine has almost evaporated then add the tomatoes, potatoes, some salt and pepper and simmer for about 5 minutes. Add the fish broth and simmer for another 5 minutes before adding the fillets. Lower the heat and simmer uncovered until it loses the watery look and the fish is cooked through, 10 minutes or so. Add the lemon juice and the chopped parsley, rock the pot to distribute it all gently and taste for salt.
Add a grind of pepper and serve hot with bread.

1 kg (2 lb 4 oz) assorted whole soup fish (small fish suitable for making stock), cleaned and gutted

a large bunch of flat-leaf parsley

⅓ celery stalk, plus 4 heaped tablespoons chopped, including some leaves

3 garlic cloves, peeled, 1 left whole and 2 chopped

1 large red onion

100 ml (3½ fl oz) olive oil

60 ml (2 fl oz/¼ cup) white wine

450 g (1 lb) very ripe tomatoes, peeled and cut into chunks

400 g (14 oz) potatoes, cut into chunks of about 1.5 cm (⅝ inch)

400 g (14 oz) perch or snapper fillet, cut into 4 pieces, or 4 x 100 g (3½ oz) fillets , all bones and skin removed

juice of 1 lemon

# GREEN BEAN &
# POTATO SOUP

The two main ingredients for this soup are abundant in Portugal —
the country has beans, beans and more beans, and they are always
lovely. And in my guide book it said: 'If you want your potatoes to
grow, you have to talk to them in Portuguese'. This makes a rather
army-style amount of thick soup that will probably give you two
days' worth — you could send some over to your neighbours if you
find you have too much, or just halve the quantities.

Halve the leeks and slice them up thinly. Put them in a bowl of water, slosh
them around with your hands to make sure there is no grit inside, and then
drain them in a colander.

Rinse the lamb or beef to get rid of any stray bits of bone and pat dry. Heat
the olive oil in a large wide pot and brown the bones well, cooking on both
sides until deep golden. Add the onion and leeks around the bones and sauté
until those too are nicely golden and well cooked. Add the garlic and cook
until you start to smell it, then add the beans, turning them through and
seasoning with about 3 teaspoons of coarse salt and some pepper.

Add about 1.5 litres (52 fl oz/6 cups) of hot water, partly cover the pan and
simmer for an hour or so, stirring a couple of times. Add the potato and
another 500 ml (17 fl oz/2 cups) or so of hot water, depending on how much
it looks like it needs. Simmer, covered, for another 30 minutes until the
potatoes are nicely soft but not collapsing.

Remove the bones and ladle out about a litre (35 fl oz/4 cups) of soup —
mainly beans and liquid, but a few potatoes to make it nice and thick. Purée
this, then return to the pot so the soup is a mixture of chunky and smooth.

Taste for seasoning and serve hot. If anyone wants to, they can pick the bones
or you can use them just for flavouring.

**SERVES MANY**

2 small leeks

about 400 g (14 oz) lamb or beef
    knuckle bones

80 ml (2½ fl oz/⅓ cup) olive oil

1 onion, chopped

2 garlic cloves, chopped

1 kg (2 lb 4 oz) green beans, topped
    and cut into short lengths

600 g (1 lb 5 oz) potatoes, peeled
    and cut into big chunks

# TOMATO SOUP
# WITH CORIANDER
# & POACHED EGG

This is a bowl of beauty and lovely in summer when tomatoes are at their best. For me, the coriander makes this but it is sometimes served without. If you were making this in true Portuguese style you'd break the eggs straight into the soup pan and poach them in there, but, if you find the thought a bit intimidating, poach them in a separate pan of water. Peel the tomatoes by scoring a cross in the base of each one, dipping them for a few seconds into a bowl of boiling water, then putting them into cold water. You will be able to peel the skin away from the cross. If you like, cut them in half and squeeze out the seeds.

Heat the oil in a stockpot and sauté the onion until golden and sticky. Add the chopped garlic and bay leaf and cook until you start to smell the garlic, then add the tomatoes. Sauté until the juices from the tomatoes reduces and they start cooking in the oil and taking the flavours from the pot. Season very generously.

Add 750 ml (26 fl oz/3 cups) of hot water and bring back to the boil. Cover the pot, lower the heat and simmer for 10 minutes. Turn off the heat, remove the bay leaf and ladle out 3 slotted spoonfuls of tomato. Purée the rest of the soup until smooth. Taste for seasoning and return the tomato chunks to the pot.

Heat enough oil to cover the bottom of a small frying pan. Fry the *chouriço* and *presunto* slices, in batches if needed, until very crisp and golden. Lift out, keeping the oil. Cut the bread into rough cubes and fry in the same oil with the squashed garlic clove until lightly golden.

To poach the eggs, add a dash of vinegar to a saucepan of lightly boiling water. Break each egg into a cup first, then slide into the water. When the water is starting to just bubble, turn the heat as low as possible, cover the pan and leave for a few minutes until set. Lift the eggs out with a slotted spoon into flat bowls, ladle soup around them and sprinkle with coriander, black pepper and salt on the egg, if you like. Serve immediately with *chouriço*, *presunto* and bread cubes in the bowl or alongside it.

**SERVES 4**

3 tablespoons olive oil, plus some extra

1 red onion, chopped

3 garlic cloves, peeled, 2 chopped and 1 slightly squashed

1 bay leaf

650 g (1 lb 7 oz) very ripe tomatoes, peeled and thickly sliced

4 thickish slices *chouriço* sausage or *linguica*

4 thinnish slices *presunto* or prosciutto

1 thick slice of bread

4 eggs, at room temperature

1 tablespoon chopped coriander (cilantro), plus a few extra leaves

# POACHED FISH
# WITH LEMON OIL

The Greeks have a wonderful way with fish, and I love this. It's delicate yet aromatic — not quite a soup. It is an easy, healthy, almost instant food that you could serve to any generation. You will need a nice big and wide pot here as there is not too much liquid and the ingredients all need to float comfortably. You can use any firm white fish fillets that won't break up too much.

Greek celery is amazing and seems to give a wonderful flavour to their soups. It is lovely clumps and small thin stalks and leaves that look almost like parsley — you might never guess that it's celery if you found it at the market.

Put the potato, carrot, zucchini, celery and onion into a wide pot and add 750 ml (26 fl oz/3 cups) of water. Season with salt. Bring to the boil and simmer uncovered for about 15 minutes. Add the fish, shuffling the vegetables if necessary to ensure that the fish is covered by broth. Simmer, uncovered, over low heat for 10–15 minutes (depending on the thickness of the fish) until the fish is cooked through but not breaking up.

For the lemon oil, whip the lemon juice and oil with a little salt in a bowl until thick and creamy. Remove the soup from the heat and discard the onion and celery. Pour in the lemon oil and rock the pot to distribute it well. Leave it for a few minutes so the flavours mingle, and check your seasoning. Scatter in the parsley. Remove the fish to a bowl and break it up into three pieces using a fork and spoon. To serve, put one piece of fish per bowl, a couple of pieces of each vegetable, a good ladleful of broth and a grind of pepper.

SERVES 3

1 large potato, peeled, halved and cut into 5 or 6 pieces

2 carrots, cut into 3 cm (1¼ inch) rounds

2 zucchini (courgettes), cut into 2–3 cm (1¼ inch) rounds

1 small celery stalk with leaves (about 60 g/2¼ oz) or a small bunch of Greek-style celery

about 40 g (1½ oz) round spring onions (scallions), white part only

1 firm boneless white fish fillet, such as ocean perch or ling (about 440 g/15½ oz)

1 tablespoon roughly chopped flat-leaf parsley

**LEMON OIL**
juice of 1 large juicy lemon

80 ml (2½ fl oz/⅓ cup) best extra virgin olive oil

# VERMICELLI SOUP
# WITH TOMATO & BASIL

This is very simple, quick and memorable when it's properly cooked. It really is my crisis-saver. If you use vegetable or chicken broth, your soup will have a stronger taste — but with just plain water like this, it is quick and beautiful and means you can present a meal in no time. Serve this immediately or the pasta just swells in the soup. If you're not feeling fantastic, or are down in the dumps with a bit of a cold, this is the thing to lift your spirits.

SERVES 4–6

Put the water, passata and basil leaves in a pan and add 1½ teaspoons of salt (this shouldn't be necessary if you're using broth). Bring to the boil, then simmer over low heat for 6–7 minutes before adding the pasta. Cook the pasta until a few seconds before the packet says it should be ready (it will continue cooking in the hot broth) and then immediately remove the pan from the heat. Ladle out into bowls, diving to the bottom of the pot each time to make sure everyone has a fair helping of pasta and broth. Drizzle a little olive oil over each bowl, if you like, but definitely give a good sprinkling of parmesan (at least 1 very heaped tablespoon for each bowl). Serve immediately.

1.75 litres (61 fl oz/7 cups) water or broth

1 tablespoon tomato passata (puréed tomatoes)

4 basil leaves

120 g (4¼ oz) vermicelli or angel hair pasta, broken up

best olive oil, to serve

grated parmesan cheese, to serve

# RED PEPPER SOUP WITH OLIVES, LEMON RIND & YOGHURT

You can add any flavours you like to the base of this soup. Here, I use fresh rosemary and serve the soup with a yoghurt, black olive and lemon flavour. You might like to use another herb like fresh basil with a swirl of cream, or try adding a good kick of chilli oil to serve. You could even add a drop of truffle oil and a couple of grilled prawns (broiled shrimp). Serve with or without the yoghurt.

SERVES 4

Preheat the grill (broiler) to high. Line a large oven tray with foil and arrange the peppers, skin side up, in a single layer. Grill for about 30 minutes until the skin has darkened in places and swelled up and the peppers are soft. You might need to move them around on the tray so they are evenly grilled or remove the halves that are blackened and leave some in for longer.

Transfer the peppers to a bowl, cover with plastic wrap (or put in a plastic bag and seal) and leave to sweat for 10 minutes to make peeling easier. Peel off the skin.

Heat the olive oil in a large saucepan and sauté the garlic and onion for about 5 minutes. Add the tomato and cook until it begins to bubble. Add the pepper halves, tearing them into large chunks as you put them in the pan. Season with salt and pepper. Add 750 ml (26 fl oz/3 cups) of water and bring to the boil, then lower the heat, cover the pan and simmer gently for about 30 minutes. Remove from the heat and purée. The soup should be fairly thick: if it seems too watery, simmer uncovered for a while longer. If it seems too thick, add a little more water. Check the seasoning and serve the soup hot with a dollop of yoghurt and a sprinkling of chopped olives, lemon rind and rosemary.

4 red peppers (capsicums), cut in half lengthways and seeded

2 tablespoons olive oil

2 garlic cloves, lightly crushed with the flat of a knife

1 small red onion, sliced

4 ripe tomatoes, peeled and chopped, or 400 g (14 oz) tinned, chopped tomatoes

300 g (10½ oz) plain Greek yoghurt

40 g (1½ oz/⅓ cup) pitted black olives, roughly chopped

finely grated rind of 1 lemon

leaves from 2 rosemary sprigs, finely chopped

# VEGETABLE SOUP

On a trip to Portugal, I went to a fruit and vegetable market in the Algarve and asked them to give me whatever vegetables a Portuguese lady would use to make a soup, please. They gave me these exact amounts for one family. When I got back to the house, my friend Teresa arrived to cook with me. And she knew exactly what to do with them. Both Teresa and the greengrocer lady said they might have put in a beef bone, too, maybe just a knuckle or two for flavour and then lifted it out. This is simple, lovely and healthy — the kind of soup I want to eat once a week forever.

SERVES 6

Heat the oil in a large pot and sauté the onion, chopped carrot and zucchini until softened. Add 1.25 litres (44 fl oz/5 cups) of cold water (enough to cover the spinach to be put in later). Season well, add the potatoes and halved carrot, stir and bring to the boil. Cover and reduce the heat a dash. Cook for 15 minutes, then check there is still enough water. Stir in the spinach, cover again, bring back to the boil and cook for 10 minutes more. The potatoes should be soft but not collapsing.

Lift out most of the potatoes and pieces of carrot with a slotted spoon, mash well and return to the pot. Stir and leave covered until ready to serve (it's best not quite piping hot). Add water if it needs thinning, but it should be more like a thin stew than a thick soup. Serve with bread.

2 tablespoons olive oil

2 white onions, chopped

2 large carrots, peeled, 1 chopped and the other halved

225 g (8 oz) zucchini (courgettes) or baby marrow, chopped

700 g (1 lb 9 oz) potatoes, peeled and thickly sliced

3 handfuls of spinach, Swiss chard (silverbeet) or kale leaves, left whole or torn if they are large

# TAHINI SOUP

This is a very simple soup that can be made in minutes. Traditionally it's from the Cycladic Islands in Greece, and is eaten in the week leading up to Easter, or on Good Friday when simple meat-free foods are eaten.

SERVES 4

Toast the sesame seeds lightly in a small dry frying pan. Add the paprika and the chilli, if using, and cook briefly, taking care not to burn them. Stir the lemon zest through then remove from the pan to a small bowl.

Bring 1 litre (35 fl oz/4 cups) of water to the boil in a pot with some salt. Add the egg noodles and boil until just tender, about 2 minutes, or according to the packet instructions if dried.

Meanwhile, put the tahini and lemon juice into a bowl, add a ladleful of the boiling noodle water and whisk until smooth. When the noodles are ready, pour the tahini mixture in and stir gently over the heat for a couple of minutes. Taste for salt. Serve in bowls with a dribble of olive oil, a scattering of the sesame paprika mixture and a grind of pepper.

2 teaspoons sesame seeds

½ teaspoon sweet paprika

sprinkling of dried ground chilli, (optional)

1 teaspoon grated lemon zest

about 150 g (5½ oz) fresh egg-free noodles or 80 g (2¾ oz) dried

135 g (4¾ oz/½ cup) tahini

juice of 1½ lemons

best olive oil, for serving

# WHITE BEAN SOUP

*Fasolada* is a wonderful wintry chunky soup from Greece. My friend Lisa brought this version to our table ready-cooked one Sunday for lunch, which I love. Depending on the beans you use, you may need to add more water. Often smaller beans are used but this is also lovely with the bigger butter beans. This was originally a poor man's dish. Cheap and filling but beloved and comforting, people would often exclaim, 'If only we had a *fasolada* now!' Use best-quality olive oil.

Cover the beans with plenty of cold water and soak overnight. The next day drain and rinse them, and put into a pot with cold water to cover. Bring to the boil, skimming off any scum that has formed. Drain and rinse again. Wipe any scum that has collected on the pot then return the beans to it. Add 2 litres (70 fl oz/8 cups) of cold water, the whole garlic clove, bay leaf, celery stalk and the onion half. Simmer, partly covered, for about an hour, until tender. Larger beans will take longer and will need more water. Add salt in the last 10 minutes or so.

Meanwhile, heat the oil in a stockpot and sauté the chopped onion (not the spring onion) until soft and golden. Add the chopped garlic and carrots and when the garlic smells good, add the tomatoes. Season with salt and pepper. Swish about 125 ml (4 fl oz/½ cup) of water in the tomato tin and pour into the pot. Put the lid on and simmer for 10 minutes or so. When the beans are ready, pick out and discard the vegetables and bay leaf then pour the beans and their water into the tomato sauce. Simmer for 10 minutes, adding a little water if it's too thick. Ladle into bowls and serve with onion, parsley and celery leaves on top, a drizzle of oil and a grind of pepper.

**SERVES 6**

500 g (1 lb 2 oz) dried butter beans (lima or cannellini, or substitute with haricot or navy beans)

3 garlic cloves, peeled, 1 left whole and 2 chopped

1 bay leaf

1 small celery stalk

½ small onion

4 tablespoons olive oil

1 large onion, chopped

3 carrots, peeled and cut into nice chunks

400 g (14 oz) tinned chopped tomatoes

50 g (1¾ oz) red onion or round spring onions (scallions), roughly chopped

½ cup very roughly chopped flat-leaf parsley

¼ cup roughly chopped celery leaves

best olive oil, to serve

# 4

~ SALADS ~

# BABY SPINACH, BRESAOLA, APPLE & NUT SALAD

*Naturally, the oil and vinegar here can be adjusted to suit your personal taste. This is a simple, healthy and nutritious salad that will serve four as a side dish and two as a light main course.*

Put the nuts in a frying pan over medium heat and dry-fry until they are lightly golden. Sprinkle with salt and leave on one side. Cut the apple into about 10 or 12 slices. Whisk together the olive oil and balsamic vinegar and season with salt and pepper.

Place all the salad ingredients in a large bowl, splash with the dressing and add any extra salt and pepper. Mix through and serve immediately.

**SERVES 4 AS A SIDE SALAD**

40 g (1½ oz/¼ cup) shelled whole almonds

20 shelled pistachio nuts

1 green apple, cored

3 tablespoons extra virgin olive oil

1 tablespoon balsamic vinegar

80 g (2¾ oz) small English spinach leaves

50 g (1¾ oz) parmesan or mature pecorino cheese shavings

50 g (1¾ oz) finely sliced *bresaola*, left whole or cut into thin strips

# GREEK SALAD

The quality of tomatoes, olive oil and the other ingredients is really important to make the kind of salad at home that one will have eaten on holiday near a sun-soaked beach. You can add a handful of other greens instead of the *glistrida* (purslane), if you like, but the padded thickness of their leaves is great, or just leave it plain. Many Greeks use only olive oil to dress their salads, while others add a little red wine vinegar. The juices at the bottom of the bowl are enjoyed and bread is used for *'papara'*, the soaking of bread in the juices before eating. In some places in Greece they serve a dollop of *mizithra* cheese on top instead of feta.

SERVES 2–4

Put the tomatoes, cucumber, onion, olives and capers into a serving bowl. Add the *glistrida* and season with a little salt and a few grinds of pepper. Put the feta on top and crumble the oregano over with your fingers. Drizzle the olive oil over, and the vinegar, if using. Serve with bread.

8 gorgeous small ripe tomatoes, quartered

1 cucumber (200 g/7 oz), sliced thickly on the diagonal

1 small–medium red onion, sliced

about 17 kalamata olives in brine, drained

1 heaped tablespoon capers

2 small handfuls of *glistrida* (purslane) if you can get it

150 g (5½ oz) slab of feta

1 teaspoon or so of dried oregano

80 ml (2½ fl oz/⅓ cup) extra virgin olive oil

1 tablespoon red wine vinegar (optional)

# CHICKPEA, FETA &
CORIANDER SALAD

This is my friend Stephen's way of serving chickpeas. It can be made beforehand and left to marinate for a couple of hours before being served at room temperature. Make sure that everything has cooled before you mix it all together, or else the feta will melt. I bought skinned chickpeas in Greece, which worked well and, if you need to be a little more spontaneous, you can use tinned chickpeas. Serve with chicken breasts or lamb chops that have been marinated in cumin and yoghurt and then grilled.

If you're using tinned chickpeas, just rinse them and put them in a bowl. Otherwise, rinse the soaked chickpeas, put them in a saucepan, cover generously with water and bring to the boil. Lower the heat slightly and cook for 1–1½ hours, until they are soft but not falling apart, adding salt towards the end of the cooking time. Leave them in their liquid if you will not be making the salad right away. When cooled, drain and put the chickpeas in a large bowl, picking out as many of the loose skins as you can. (You can put them in a colander and shake roughly or rub them around with your hands, then pick out the skins.)

Heat 3 tablespoons of the olive oil and fry the red onion gently until it is cooked through and lightly golden. Add the garlic and chilli and cook for a few more seconds until you can smell the garlic. Take care not to brown the garlic. Leave to cool completely.

Add the feta, spring onion, coriander, parsley and lemon juice to the chickpeas and season with pepper and a dash more salt, if needed. Add the cooled garlic oil and the remaining olive oil and mix through very well.

**SERVES 6 AS A SIDE DISH**

250 g (9 oz/1¼ cups) dried chickpeas (without skins if possible), soaked overnight in cold water, or 400 g (14 oz) tinned chickpeas

250 ml (9 fl oz/1 cup) olive oil

1 large red onion, chopped

5 garlic cloves, very finely chopped

1 or 2 red chillies, seeded and finely chopped

250 g (9 oz) crumbled feta cheese

4 spring onions (scallions), green parts only, chopped

25 g (1 oz/½ cup) chopped coriander (cilantro)

30 g (1 oz/1 cup) chopped flat-leaf parsley

juice of 1 lemon

# CODDLED EGG & ANCHOVY SALAD

This is how my friend Jo makes her salad. She is an exceptional cook, full of enthusiasm and fun. She says she also likes this dressing with warm asparagus, broad beans and peas. I find it also goes well with olives and fresh raw vegetables for dunking into the sauce, or just with a plain steak and some fat chips for dipping. This will make a couple of cups of dressing that you can use as you like.

Bring about 750 ml (26 fl oz/3 cups) of salted water to the boil and dunk the rosemary and garlic in the water a few times to soften them slightly. Strip the rosemary leaves off the stem and chop very finely with the garlic. Put in a bowl.

Whisk in the anchovies, mustard and lemon juice, a few grindings of black pepper and a little of each of the oils. Whisk well until it all comes together, a bit like mayonnaise.

Meanwhile, lower the eggs into the boiling water and boil for 3 minutes. (To be perfect, all of the white and a fine layer of yolk should be set; the rest of the yolk should be soft.) Rinse under cold water until cool enough to peel. Add to the dressing, whisking to break the eggs into small bits. Add the rest of the oil, whisking continuously until completely combined. Whisk in a teaspoonful of warm water to finish the dressing.

Put all the salad ingredients in a large bowl. Splash the dressing over the top, tossing well so that all the leaves carry a heavy coating of dressing, and serve immediately.

SERVES 6

## DRESSING
2 soft rosemary sprigs, rinsed

2 garlic cloves

about 8 anchovy fillets packed in oil, drained and chopped

1 heaped tablespoon dijon mustard

2 tablespoons lemon juice

90 ml (3 fl oz) vegetable oil

90 ml (3 fl oz) olive oil

2 eggs, at room temperature

## SALAD
1 fennel bulb, halved and very finely sliced

about 100 g (3½ oz) radicchio or treviso, torn into large chunks

about 250 g (9 oz) firm inner lettuce leaves

2 celery stalks, finely sliced

# BLACK-EYED BEAN SALAD

I have had this salad served as a bed for some fried salt cod, but it would be delicious with almost anything. If you have leftovers for the next day you might like to moisten the beans with a touch more dressing.

SERVES 4–6

Cover the beans with plenty of water and soak overnight. Drain the beans, put them in a large pot and cover with fresh water. Bring to the boil, skimming off any scum that rises to the top, then lower the heat slightly and cook for about 35 minutes until soft but not mushy. Drain the beans again, then leave to cool in the colander before tipping into a serving bowl.

Heat 2 tablespoons of the oil in a small pan and sauté the shallots until golden. Add the peppers and cook until they are softened and turning golden but not dark. Add the garlic and sauté for 1 minute until you start to smell it, then turn off the heat. Stir in the parsley then add the mixture to the beans in the bowl.

Mix together the remaining olive oil, the vinegar, lemon juice and piri piri. Season well with salt and pepper and pour over the bean salad. Toss well before serving.

500 g (1 lb 2 oz) dried black-eyed beans

about 5 tablespoons olive oil

3 shallots or 1 onion, chopped

1 small red pepper (capsicum), seeded and chopped

1 small green pepper (capsicum), seeded and chopped

3–4 garlic cloves, chopped

4 tablespoons chopped flat-leaf parsley

1 tablespoon red wine vinegar

juice of 1 lemon

a good pinch of ground piri piri

# CABBAGE & PEPPER SALAD

If this amount seems crazy, then just make half a portion. It's a lovely huge amount to make though, and it keeps well in the fridge, covered for five to six days after it has been made. It will need a few days first in the fridge to drag out the juices before you can eat it. The red and green peppers used for this are the small, long and thin Greek ones.

SERVES MANY, MANY

Discard the outer leaves of the cabbage. Halve and core it, then shred into medium-fine slices. Put the cabbage in a large bowl with everything else except the olive oil and lemons. Roll up your sleeves and mix and knead everything together well with your hands. It needs a lot of pressing about. Cover and leave in the fridge for three days before tasting. But in the meantime turn it through each day to drag all the juices out.

Serve the salad drizzled with olive oil and a squeeze of lemon juice if you like.

1 small cabbage (1.2 kg/2 lb 10 oz)

400 g (14 oz) carrots, coarsely grated

400 g (14 oz) small green sweet peppers (capsicums), seeded and sliced

400 g (14 oz) small red sweet peppers (capsicums), seeded and sliced

50 g (1¾ oz) Greek celery (or thin young celery stalks with some leaves), chopped

180 ml (6 fl oz) red wine vinegar

3 tablespoons salt

3 garlic cloves, chopped

generous pinch of dried ground chillies

extra virgin olive oil, to serve

lemon quarters, to serve

# 5

~ PASTA, GNOCCHI
& RICE ~

# SPAGHETTI WITH TOMATO & SCAMPI

In the restaurants of Venice, the scampi (langoustines) are sometimes served whole with the shells and heads intact. It certainly looks impressive, but can be difficult to eat, so you decide whether you want to peel them. I recommend seeking out small-ish scampi and keeping the heads on for flavour but peeling the bodies for easier eating. Some small scampi are quite easy to peel once they've been cooked, so they would be fine to serve with the shells intact.

First, clean the scampi. Remove the shells from the bodies and devein (and remove the heads if you prefer), rinse and set aside.

Heat 2 tablespoons of oil in a pan and sauté the onion until completely softened, stirring often. Add the tomatoes, a pinch of dried ground chilli and some salt. Simmer, uncovered, for 10–15 minutes, squashing the tomatoes down with a wooden spoon occasionally, until the tomatoes melt and are free of lumps and you have a nice sauce. Keep warm.

Heat the butter and the last tablespoon of the olive oil in a large non-stick frying pan. When hot, add the scampi and bay leaf and sauté over very high heat until the base of the scampi becomes golden and forms a bit of a crust. Turn the scampi over and add a dash of salt, a pinch of dried ground chilli and then the garlic. Now add the parsley. Continue cooking the scampi until you can smell the garlic and both sides of the scampi are just cooked, then pour in the prosecco (or white wine if you don't have prosecco) and simmer rapidly until it has evaporated. The scampi meat must be soft but not overcooked.

Meanwhile, cook the pasta in boiling salted water until tender. Drain, reserving a dash of the cooking water in case it's needed to loosen the sauce. Add the spaghetti to the scampi pan and scrape the tomato into the pan as well. Toss everything together as gently as possible, preferably by flicking the pan to coat all and not mash things up. Add some of the reserved pasta cooking water if it seems too dry. Serve at once, with black pepper.

**SERVES 2**

8 smallish scampi (langoustines, red-claw or large prawns/shrimp) with heads (about 6–7 cm/2½ inches)

60 ml (2 fl oz/¼ cup) olive oil

½ small white onion, finely chopped

250 g (9 oz/1 cup) peeled tinned or chopped fresh tomatoes

2 good pinches of dried ground chilli

1 tablespoon butter

1 bay leaf

2 garlic cloves, chopped

1 heaped tablespoon chopped flat-leaf parsley

60 ml (2 fl oz/¼ cup) prosecco

160 g (5½ oz) thick spaghetti

# PENNE WITH PRAWNS, CREAM & TOMATO

This is simple and not too rich. I use Calvados just because I liked the way it turned out once when I didn't have my usual brandy. The prawns here are not too many — so you can pick them out at the end and serve more to some, less to others. And there is just a little cream, to sweeten things up even more …

SERVES 3

Melt half of the butter in a smallish pan and, when it is sizzling, add the tomatoes. Season with salt and a dash of pepper and then cook over medium heat for about 10 minutes, until it is thick.

Cook the pasta in a large pan of boiling salted water, following the packet instructions. Meanwhile, heat a large non-stick frying pan over high heat. Add the oil and the rest of the butter and, when it is sizzling, add the prawns and garlic. Over the highest heat possible, cook the prawns until they are quite bright and the undersides are golden and crusty in places. It is important that the heat is high and that you have a non-stick pan, so that the prawns fry quickly rather than boil in their own liquid. Turn them with tongs and, when they are cooked, scatter them with salt. Add the Calvados and cook until it evaporates.

Drain the pasta, keeping a cupful of the cooking water. Add the tomato sauce to the prawns, along with the cream and parsley. Heat until just bubbling. Add the pasta and toss well. If it seems like you need it, add a little of the cooking water to help the sauce coat the pasta. Serve immediately with a grinding of pepper.

40 g (1½ oz) butter

200 g (7 oz) tinned tomatoes with juice, puréed

250 g (9 oz) penne

2 teaspoons olive oil

500 g (1 lb 2 oz) raw prawns (shrimp), peeled and deveined

2 garlic cloves, peeled and squashed a bit

2 tablespoons Calvados (apple brandy)

2½ tablespoons thin (pouring) cream

1 tablespoon chopped flat-leaf parsley

# PASTA WITH SARDINES & WILD FENNEL

This is lovely and quite delicate in its simplicity. It will make six filling portions. Use small sardines, up to about 12 cm (4½ inches) long and around 30 g (1 oz) each. If you like a stronger taste, you could also add a few mashed-up anchovies. You will need a large handful of beautiful soft wild fennel here.

Fillet each sardine by cutting off the head and making a slit along the underside with a small sharp knife. Remove the guts, then remove the central bone by pulling it away by the tail with one hand while holding the sardine with the other. You will be left with two attached fillets.

Remove any tough stalks from the fennel, leaving them in wisps or breaking them up if they are very long. Crumble the bread into coarse crumbs. Heat 3 tablespoons of the olive oil in a non-stick frying pan and fry the crumbs until they are deep golden and crisp. Remove to a small bowl. Cook the pasta in a large pan of boiling salted water, following the packet instructions.

Heat the remaining olive oil in a large non-stick frying pan. Add the garlic, fennel and spring onion and sauté for a few seconds to flavour the oil, then add the sardines. Continue to cook for a few minutes over a high heat, flipping them around in the pan, but taking care not to break them up. Cook for a couple of minutes until the fish are just opaque. Remove from the heat until your pasta is ready.

Drain the pasta but keep a cup or so of the cooking water. Add the pasta to the frying pan if it fits, if not, transfer the pasta and sardines to a large bowl and carefully toss together, adding some of the pasta cooking water if necessary. Serve immediately with a small handful of breadcrumbs and a grinding of black pepper over each bowl.

**SERVES 6**

about 1 kg (2 lb 4 oz) small fresh sardines

1 large handful of wild fennel or baby fennel fronds

3 slices of white bread, crusts removed

185 ml (6 fl oz/¾ cup) olive oil

500 g (1 lb 2 oz) linguini

2 garlic cloves, lightly crushed with the flat of a knife

1 spring onion (scallion), white part only, finely sliced

# SPAGHETTI & MEATBALLS

If you're organised, you could make the meatballs in tomato sauce the day before and just heat them up while you're cooking the pasta. Once you have fried the meatballs, you will have some nice tasty oil with meaty bits in the saucepan. I like to sauté some just-parboiled spinach or even potatoes in this until they have mingled with the pan oil and drunk up the flavour. Serve the spinach as a side dish and then all you need is a couple of small scoops of ice cream for dessert and you're settled.

For the meatballs, soak the bread in the milk in a small bowl, squishing it through your fingers so that it breaks up completely.

Put the mince in a large bowl with the parsley, cinnamon, cumin, the bread mixture and the salt. Grate in the onion (it is easier to do this holding the whole onion and then keeping the unused half for another time). Mix everything together thoroughly, kneading it with your hands as though it were a bread dough. Form about 25 small meatballs the size of large cherry tomatoes, rolling them between your palms so they are compact and smooth. Keep the made ones on a plate while you finish rolling the rest. Depending on their age, kids might like to help you with the rolling.

Heat the light olive oil in a non-stick frying pan and fry the meatballs in batches, making sure they are golden before you turn them. You should be able to shuffle them by holding the handle of the pan and giving a good flick with your wrist. If not, use tongs to turn them.

Meanwhile, make the sauce. Heat the oil in a large saucepan big enough to eventually hold the meatballs. Add the garlic cloves and, when you can smell them, add the tomatoes. Season with salt, add the basil and simmer for 10 minutes or so. Break up the tomatoes with a wooden spoon as you stir from time to time.

When all the meatballs have been fried, add them to the tomato sauce and stir in just under 250 ml (9 fl oz/1 cup) of water. Simmer uncovered for another 20–25 minutes, adding another splash of water if needed, until the meatballs are soft and there is a fair amount of thickened sauce to toss into your pasta. Taste for salt, adjusting if necessary.

Cook the spaghetti in boiling salted water, following the packet instructions. Drain, return to the cooking pot and gently but thoroughly toss the butter through. Serve the pasta in individual bowls with a good ladleful of the tomato sauce, a few meatballs and a scattering of parmesan on top.

SERVES 4

**MEATBALLS**
40–50 g (1½–1¾ oz) soft crustless white bread, torn into chunks
80 ml (2½ fl oz/⅓ cup) milk
400 g (14 oz) minced (ground) pork and beef
2 tablespoons chopped flat-leaf parsley
½ teaspoon ground cinnamon
½ teaspoon ground cumin
½ teaspoon salt
½ small red onion
about 80 ml (2½ fl oz/⅓ cup) light olive oil, for frying

**SAUCE**
2 tablespoons olive oil
2 garlic cloves, peeled and squashed a bit
400 g (14 oz) tinned chopped tomatoes
3–4 basil leaves, torn
250 ml (9 fl oz/1 cup)

350 g (12 oz) spaghetti
30 g (1 oz) butter
grated parmesan cheese, to serve

# SPINACH & RICOTTA CANNELLONI

I learnt to make these with my brother and sister-in-law, Luca and Luisa. They really are amazing proper Italian cooks, who put this together effortlessly, as though they were just ironing a shirt. Sometimes they use fresh egg pasta squares instead of the crepes, boiling them first to soften and laying them out on clean tea towels to dry. Although this might seem a bit fiddly, it's worth it in the end because you can just take this one lovely dish to the table.

If you want to break up the workload a bit, fry the crepes and make the tomato sauce and spinach mix in advance, keeping them covered until you are ready to use them. Then, at the last moment, you can heat up your oven, make the béchamel, fill and roll the crepes, dot the béchamel and tomatoes over the top, and bake. Your oven dish needs to be about 30 x 20 cm (12 x 8 inches) so that you can fit 12 rolled crepes in two rows. If the rolled crepes won't quite fit your dish, you can trim off their ends — it is a little fiddly, but they do look very smart that way.

For the crepes, whisk the eggs in a bowl and then whisk in the flour and a couple of pinches of salt. Add the butter, still whisking, and then slowly incorporate the milk to make a smooth batter. Leave it to stand for 20 minutes or so.

Heat a little butter in a 15 cm (6 inch) non-stick frying pan. Add half a ladleful of batter and quickly swirl the pan around so the batter covers it as evenly as possible. Cook until the underneath is golden, then flip the crepe over with a spatula and cook the other side. Move to a plate with the spatula and cook the rest of the batter. You will need 12 crepes and you should have enough mixture to allow for a couple of disasters.

continues on next page …

**SERVES 6**

**CREPES**
**3 eggs**
**150 g (5½ oz) plain (all-purpose) flour**
**50 g (1¾ oz) butter, melted, plus extra butter for frying**
**250 ml (9 fl oz/1 cup) milk**

continues on next page …

For the tomato sauce, heat the garlic with the oil in a saucepan and, when you begin to smell the garlic, add the tomatoes. Season with salt, bring to the boil, then lower the heat and simmer for about 15 minutes until the tomatoes have melted. Add the basil and 125 ml (4 fl oz/½ cup) of water towards the end of this time. Purée to a smooth sauce.

For the filling, rinse the spinach under cold water, shake off the excess and then put in a saucepan with just the water clinging to the leaves. Cook over medium–low heat, turning with a wooden spoon, until the leaves have wilted. Cool a little and then squeeze out as much water as you can and chop the spinach. Put the spinach in a bowl with the ricotta, egg, parmesan, nutmeg and salt and pepper to taste. Mix well.

To make the béchamel, melt the butter in a small saucepan. Whisk in the flour and cook for a few minutes, stirring constantly, then begin adding the warm milk. It will be immediately absorbed, so work quickly, whisking with one hand while adding ladlefuls of milk with the other. When the sauce seems to be smooth and not too stiff, add salt, pepper and a grating of nutmeg and continue cooking, even after it comes to the boil, for 5 minutes or so, mixing all the time. It should be a very thick and smooth sauce.

Meanwhile, preheat the oven to 180°C (350°F/Gas 4) and grease a 30 x 20 cm (12 x 8 inch) baking dish. To put together, dollop some béchamel in the bottom of the dish and rock it from side to side so that the béchamel thinly covers the bottom. Spoon a couple of tablespoons of filling along one side of a crepe and then roll it up tightly. Repeat with all the crepes and lay them on the béchamel like soldiers in two rows of six. Pour the rest of the béchamel over the top, then dot generously with the tomato sauce. Sprinkle with the parmesan and bake for about 40 minutes, until golden and bubbling nicely. Let it cool a dash before serving, then check carefully where each crepe begins and ends and lift them out with an egg slice.

**TOMATO SAUCE**
1 garlic clove, peeled and squashed
   a bit
2 tablespoons olive oil
400 g (14 oz) tinned diced tomatoes
about 4 basil leaves

**FILLING**
300 g (10½ oz) English spinach
   leaves, roughly chopped
500 g (1 lb 2 oz) fresh ricotta
1 egg, lightly beaten
80 g (2¾ oz) grated parmesan cheese
freshly grated nutmeg

**BÉCHAMEL SAUCE**
60 g (2¼ oz) butter
40 g (1½ oz) plain (all-purpose)
   flour
550 ml (19 fl oz) milk, warmed
freshly grated nutmeg

50 g (1¾ oz/⅓ cup) grated parmesan
   cheese

# TWO LASAGNES

**MEAT LASAGNE**

My mother makes a good lasagne — and she isn't Italian. She mostly uses the dried 'ready-to-cook' sheets and sometimes adds chopped celery, peppers (capsicums) and mushrooms to the meat sauce. The ready-to-cook sheets do absorb quite a lot of liquid, so it's important to keep your sauces fairly runny. If you prefer, just use the sheets that need boiling beforehand. The meat sauce and béchamel can be made in advance. I often make huge pots of the minced meat sauce and freeze it; then when I want to make lasagne it doesn't seem much of a job at all.

For the meat sauce, heat the olive oil in a large saucepan and sauté the onion over medium heat until it is quite golden. Stir in the garlic then add the mince, bay leaves, cinnamon stick, worcestershire sauce, mint and paprika. Sauté over high heat for 8–10 minutes until the meat starts to brown, stirring often to prevent sticking. Add the wine and cook for 5 minutes or so until it evaporates. Add the tomatoes, cook for a few minutes and then add 750 ml (26 fl oz/3 cups) of water. Season with salt. Bring to the boil, lower the heat and simmer uncovered for 1 hour. Add the parsley for the last 10 minutes.

To make the béchamel, melt the butter in a small saucepan. Whisk in the flour and cook for a few minutes, stirring constantly, then begin adding the warm milk. It will be immediately absorbed, so work quickly, whisking with one hand while adding ladlefuls of milk with the other. When the sauce seems to be smooth and not too stiff, add salt, pepper and a grating of nutmeg and continue cooking, even after it comes to the boil, for 5 minutes or so, mixing all the time. It should be a very thick and smooth sauce.

Preheat the oven to 180°C (350°F/Gas 4) and grease a deep 30 x 22 cm (12 x 8½ inch) baking dish. Drizzle some béchamel over the bottom of the dish and rock it from side to side so that the béchamel more or less covers the bottom very thinly. Put a slightly overlapping layer of lasagne sheets on top. Ladle on a thin layer of meat sauce, spreading it with the back of the ladle. Add about two ladlefuls of béchamel in long drizzles and then cover with a sprinkling of grated parmesan cheese.

Add another layer of lasagne sheets, then meat sauce, béchamel and parmesan, as before, and repeat this layering twice more. Use up all the meat sauce in a last layer, then top this with a final layer of pasta. Scrape out the last of the béchamel to thinly cover the lasagne sheets and sprinkle the top with any remaining parmesan. Put in the oven with a tray underneath to catch the drips and bake for 30–40 minutes, until it is crusty in parts, golden and bubbling.

**SERVES 6–8**

**MEAT SAUCE**

125 ml (4 fl oz/½ cup) olive oil

3 onions, chopped

2 garlic cloves, finely chopped

1 kg (2 lb 4 oz) minced (ground) beef

2 bay leaves

1 cinnamon stick

2 tablespoons worcestershire sauce

1 teaspoon dried mint

2 teaspoons sweet paprika

375 ml (13 fl oz/1½ cups) white wine

800 g (1 lb 12 oz) tinned chopped tomatoes

a small bunch of flat-leaf parsley, chopped

**BÉCHAMEL SAUCE**

120 g (4¼ oz) butter

80 g (2¾ oz) plain (all-purpose) flour

1 litre (35 fl oz/4 cups) milk, warmed

freshly grated nutmeg

about 350 g (12 oz) lasagne sheets

80 g (2¾ oz) grated parmesan cheese

## TOMATO LASAGNE

This is a straightforward recipe to which you can add a few blobs of goat's cheese, some dollops of pesto, a little cooked spinach or grilled long slices of zucchini (courgette) between the layers. This is just lasagne sheets, a good tomato sauce and béchamel, and my children love it. The easiest thing is to buy dried 'ready-to-cook' pasta sheets that can be put directly into your dish (see the introduction on page 113). If you prefer, use the sheets that require boiling first.

For the tomato sauce, heat the oil and garlic in a large pan. When you begin to smell the garlic, add the tomatoes and a good pinch of salt and bring to the boil. Lower the heat and cook uncovered for about 20–25 minutes, until it has all merged into a sauce. Add the basil and 250 ml (9 fl oz/1 cup) of hot water towards the end of the cooking time. Purée until smooth, minus the garlic if you'd prefer.

To make the béchamel, melt the butter in a small saucepan. Whisk in the flour and cook for a few minutes, stirring constantly, then begin adding the warm milk. It will be immediately absorbed, so work quickly, whisking with one hand while adding ladlefuls of milk with the other. When the sauce seems to be smooth and not too stiff, add salt, pepper and a grating of nutmeg and continue cooking, even after it comes to the boil, for 5 minutes or so, mixing all the time. It should be a very thick and smooth sauce.

Preheat the oven to 180°C (350°F/Gas 4) and grease a deep 30 x 22 cm (12 x 8½ inch) baking dish. Drizzle some béchamel over the bottom of the dish to cover it very thinly. Put a slightly overlapping layer of lasagne sheets on top. Dollop a thin layer of tomato sauce over that, spreading it with the back of the ladle. Add about two ladlefuls of béchamel in long drizzles and then cover with a sprinkling of parmesan. Add another layer of lasagne sheets, then tomato, béchamel and parmesan as before, and then repeat the layers one more time. You should have about 3 tablespoons of tomato sauce and a good amount of béchamel left. Make a final layer of lasagne sheets and cover with all the remaining béchamel. Dollop the tomato sauce here and there and sprinkle with any remaining parmesan. Bake for about 30 minutes, or until it is bubbling and golden on top.

SERVES 6–8

**TOMATO SAUCE**
125 ml (4 fl oz/½ cup) olive oil
3 garlic cloves, peeled but left whole
1.2 kg (2 lb 10 oz) tinned chopped tomatoes
about 12 basil leaves, torn

**BÉCHAMEL SAUCE**
120 g (4¼ oz) butter
80 g (2¾ oz) plain (all-purpose) flour
1 litre (35 fl oz/4 cups) milk, warmed
freshly grated nutmeg
about 350 g (12 oz) lasagne sheets
80 g (2¾ oz) grated parmesan cheese

# SPAGHETTI WITH CLAMS & CALAMARI

The important thing here is timing: the calamari has to be tender and you need the seafood cooking while you par-cook the spaghetti. Then they can be tossed together at the right moment and the spaghetti can finish off its cooking in the lovely thick seafood sauce. I like to use *vongole veraci* (carpet shell clams). Your clams will probably have been purged of sand already but check with the fishmonger, otherwise you'll need to soak them for a day in well-salted water, changing the water several times.

SERVES 2

If you've been soaking your clams, give them a swirl in the water, rinse them, drain and leave in the colander. To prepare the calamari, firmly pull the head and innards from the body and wash the body well. Cut off the head just below the eyes, leaving the tentacles in one piece if they're small. Discard the head, pull the transparent quill out of the body and rinse out the tube. Peel off the outer membrane and slice the tube into slices about 3 mm (1/8 inch) thick. Pat dry with paper towel (you should have about 170 g/6 oz of cleaned calamari).

Meanwhile, heat 2 tablespoons of the olive oil in a frying pan that has a lid. Add half the garlic and, when it smells good, add the clams, 1 tablespoon of the parsley and 3 tablespoons of the white wine. Cover and cook over high heat until the clams open. Discard any that refuse to open. Transfer the clams to a large bowl, removing the shells from half of them. Add all the clam cooking water to the bowl (if you have any suspicions there may be sand in the water you can strain it through a muslin-lined colander). Wipe out the pan with paper towel.

Heat the remaining oil in the pan with the rest of the garlic. Add the calamari, 1 tablespoon of parsley, a pinch of dried ground chilli and a dash of salt. Cook over high heat until the calamari changes colour. Add the rest of the wine and let it reduce a little. Remove from the heat and return the clams and juices to the calamari pan.

Meanwhile, cook the spaghetti in boiling salted water until almost ready. Drain, add to the seafood pan and toss over high heat to thicken the clam sauce until it coats the spaghetti. Serve with olive oil, black pepper and parsley.

350 g (12 oz) clams in shells

2 calamari

80 ml (2½ fl oz/⅓ cup) olive oil

2 garlic cloves, chopped

3 tablespoons chopped flat-leaf parsley

125 ml (4 fl oz/½ cup) white wine

a pinch of dried ground chilli

best olive oil, to serve

140 g (5 oz) spaghetti

# PASTA WITH TUNA, TOMATO & OLIVES

Olives may or may not be appreciated by young ones, so I just add a few, leaving them in big chunks so anyone who doesn't like them can easily pick them out. I like to use penne, farfalle or spaghetti with this sauce. Adults can also sprinkle a little chopped chilli or chilli oil over theirs.

**SERVES 4**

Heat the oil and garlic in a wide saucepan. When you can smell the garlic, add the celery and sauté over gentle heat until it softens and turns pale gold. Add the tomatoes, season with salt and a twist of pepper and simmer for 10–15 minutes, breaking up the tomatoes with a wooden spoon. Add the tuna, breaking up the chunks with your wooden spoon. Add 3 tablespoons of hot water, let it come to the boil and then stir in the basil, parsley and olives. Simmer for a few minutes before removing from the heat. The sauce should not be too dry, so add a few more drops of water if necessary.

Cook the pasta in a large pan of boiling salted water, following the packet instructions. Drain, keeping a cupful of the cooking water. Toss the pasta with the sauce, adding a little of the cooking water if necessary to help the sauce coat the pasta. Serve immediately, with a drizzle of olive oil and a little black pepper for the adults.

2 tablespoons olive oil, plus extra to serve

2 garlic cloves, peeled and squashed a bit

25 g (1 oz) leafy celery stalks, finely chopped

400 g (14 oz) tinned chopped tomatoes

185 g (6½ oz) tuna in oil, drained

3 basil leaves, torn

1½ tablespoons finely chopped flat-leaf parsley

8 pitted kalamata olives, halved

400 g (14 oz) pasta (penne, farfalle or spaghetti)

# SPAGHETTINI WITH EGG & TOASTED PARSLEY BREADCRUMBS

This is nice and simple. The anchovies and garlic can be left out, and you could also add baby capers or maybe some chopped olives. This could nicely precede a simple sautéed chicken breast or fish fillet.

Bring a large pot of salted water to the boil. Add the eggs and boil for 4 minutes. Fish out the eggs with a slotted spoon, run under cold water and peel off the shells. Put the eggs in a large serving bowl and mash up into small bits with a fork. Add a couple of tablespoons of the olive oil and a little salt.

Add the spaghettini to the boiling water and cook, following the packet instructions. Meanwhile, heat 2 tablespoons of oil in a non-stick frying pan, then add the breadcrumbs, anchovies and garlic and sauté over medium heat until the breadcrumbs are golden and crisp. Remove from the heat and stir in the parsley and lemon zest.

Drain the spaghettini, keeping some of the cooking water. Add the pasta to the egg with a few spoonfuls of the cooking water. Toss through very well and serve immediately. Drizzle each serving with some olive oil and scatter parsley breadcrumbs over the top. Pass around the parmesan, and some black pepper for those who like it.

**SERVES 4**

4 eggs, at room temperature

4 tablespoons olive oil,
    plus extra to serve

300 g (10½ oz) spaghettini

60 g (2¼ oz) soft white bread,
    broken up into coarse crumbs

2 anchovy fillets packed in oil, finely
    chopped

1 garlic clove, finely chopped

1 heaped tablespoon chopped
    flat-leaf parsley

finely grated zest of ½ a lemon

grated parmesan cheese, to serve

# SPAGHETTI WITH SQUID INK

This is an aesthetically dramatic dish — jet black — which is how I like it, but if you prefer a softer look, add less squid ink. If your squid doesn't come with an ink sac or if it doesn't yield much ink, you can use a sachet of squid ink. These are sold by some fishmongers and delicatessens, often in a package containing two sachets of 4 g (⅛ oz) per packet. You should only need to use one sachet here, but you can add another one if you want the result to be blacker. Alternatively, you can make the sauce without any squid ink at all and mix it with black ready-made squid ink spaghetti.

**SERVES 2**

300 g (10½ oz) squid, with ink sac
60 ml (2 fl oz/¼ cup) olive oil
2 garlic cloves, chopped
a pinch of dried ground chilli
1 tablespoon chopped flat-leaf
 parsley, plus extra for serving
125 ml (4 fl oz/½ cup) white wine
140 g (5 oz) spaghetti

To prepare the squid, pull the head and innards from the body. Separate the ink sac from the rest of the innards without puncturing, then rinse gently and put in a bowl. Wash the body. Cut off the head just below the eyes, leaving the tentacles in one piece, and discard the head. Pull out the transparent quill, rinse the tube and peel off the outer membrane. Cut the squid body into 6 mm (¼ inch) strips and the tentacles into pieces. Pat dry with paper towel.

Heat the oil in a non-stick frying pan that has a lid and add the squid. Cook over high heat until the liquid begins to evaporate, then add the garlic, dried ground chilli and parsley and season with salt and pepper. When you can smell the garlic, add the wine and bring it to a simmer. Once it is bubbling up, cover with the lid, lower the heat and simmer for 10–15 minutes until most of the liquid has been absorbed.

Cut the ink sac into a cup and mix with 185 ml (6 fl oz/¾ cup) water. Pour into the pan. Add a little more water to rinse out the inky cup, pouring it into the pan. Cover and simmer for 15 minutes or until the squid is tender (check it's not drying out and add water if necessary). Taste for salt.

Meanwhile, cook the pasta in boiling salted water until tender. Drain, reserving half a cup of the cooking water. Add the pasta and cooking water to the pan with the squid and toss well to coat with the sauce. Serve with a little extra parsley and a good grind of black pepper, even though you won't see it!

# PUMPKIN GNOCCHI

I learnt to make these from my friend Julia. This pumpkin gnocchi is made without potato and is wonderfully soft and sweet. You will not be able to roll out the puréed vegetable as you would with potato gnocchi; instead use two spoons to form quenelles. The amount of flour is very approximate here and will depend entirely on how much liquid your pumpkin contains. The quality of the pumpkin is really important, so choose a sweet, bright orange one. When cooking, you need to cook and dry out your pumpkin well at the start without crisping it too much.

**SERVES 4**

Preheat your oven to 180°C (350°F/Gas 4). Line a baking tray with foil. Peel the pumpkin and remove the seeds. Cut the flesh into largish slices. Roast the pumpkin on the tray for about 30 minutes until tender but not too browned (or they will be difficult to purée). Transfer to a plate and cool a little.

Purée all the slightly warm pumpkin as smoothly as possible so it is evenly coloured and there are no chunks in the finished gnocchi. Scrape into a bowl, add the egg and salt and mix well. Add the flour, mixing it in well (try to put in as little as possible), until you have a mixture that holds its shape on a spoon.

Bring a pot of salted water to the boil. Pour some oil into a cup. If you are not going to be serving your gnocchi at once, have a slightly oiled or buttered tray ready so they won't all stick together while they wait.

Put the butter and sage in a small frying pan and heat until the butter turns golden and the sage becomes crisp, but be careful not to let them burn.

When the water is boiling, lightly dip two teaspoons in the oil, then form quenelles by passing the pumpkin back and forth between the spoons. Gently lower the gnocchi into the water then lift out with a slotted spoon when they bob up to the top. Put them in the heated butter or on your oiled tray.

Sauté the gnocchi in the hot butter for a moment or so. Spoon onto plates, dribbling the sage butter over and around. Serve immediately with nutmeg, parmesan and black pepper.

1.1 kg (2 lb 7 oz) pumpkin
   (winter squash)
1 egg, lightly beaten
about ½ teaspoon salt
about 200 g (7 oz) plain
   (all-purpose) flour
oil, for dipping
125 g (4½ oz) butter
2–3 sage sprigs
a good grating of nutmeg
lots of grated parmesan cheese

# BEETROOT GNOCCHI

The beetroot here is mainly for its uplifting colour. These gnocchi are also very good with just a blob of butter on each serving and a handful of grated parmesan scattered over. The colour pales a little when the gnocchi are boiled, but then seems to win its strength back almost immediately.

Bring a large pan of salted water to the boil, add the potatoes and boil for about 25 minutes until they are soft. Drain and, when they are cool enough to handle, peel them and pass them through a potato mill into a bowl, or mash thoroughly.

Purée the beetroot in a food processor or blender until it is absolutely, totally smooth (you will need just over half a cup of purée). Fold the purée into the potatoes, then add the flour, parmesan, egg and salt to taste. Mix first with a wooden spoon and then by hand until you have a completely smooth soft dough. The gnocchi need to be shaped and cooked straightaway to avoid your having to add more flour, which would make them hard.

Chop up the basil leaves quite roughly and chop most of the pine nuts, leaving a few whole. Put them in a bowl, add the parmesan and olive oil and mix through. You could add a dash of salt and a grind of pepper if you like. Bring a large pan of salted water to the boil and have ready a flattish dish ready with the blobs of butter in the bottom.

Divide the dough into four and roll out each portion into a long salami about 1.5 cm (⅝ inch) in diameter. Try to avoid adding flour to your work surface, but you may need to lightly flour your hands. Cut each salami into short lengths (say, 1 cm/½ inch) and don't worry if they are all different shapes and don't look completely perfect. Cook them in two batches — drop them into the boiling water and give a gentle stir. They are ready as soon as they bob up to the surface (this will only take about half a minute). Quickly lift them out with a slotted spoon, put them in the dish and toss them in the butter. Drizzle the basil dressing all over and sprinkle with parmesan. Serve immediately.

SERVES 4

**GNOCCHI**
500 g (1 lb 2 oz) potatoes, scrubbed but not peeled

1 small beetroot (beet) (about 120 g/4¼ oz), steamed and peeled

200 g (7 oz) plain (all-purpose) flour

50 g (1¾ oz/⅓ cup) grated parmesan cheese

1 egg, lightly beaten

**TO SERVE**
12 large basil leaves

30 g (1 oz) pine nuts, lightly toasted

2 tablespoons grated parmesan cheese

120 ml (4 fl oz) olive oil

4 good blobs of butter

grated parmesan cheese, to serve

# SCAMPI & GNOCCHI

This will serve four to six people, depending on what else you're serving at the table. In Italy we get potatoes that say on the bag they are perfect for gnocchi. If that doesn't happen where you live, try to choose floury potatoes of a uniform size so they will all cook to more or less the same softness at the same time.

First, clean the scampi. Peel, remove the heads and devein. Cut up the flesh into 3 or 4 pieces. Rinse, pat dry and set aside.

To make the tomato sauce, put the tomatoes in a blender or food processor and pulse until quite smooth. Heat the oil in a large frying pan and sauté the onion until it softens and is pale golden but well cooked. Add the garlic and, when you can smell it, add the wine and let it bubble up until it has evaporated and the onion is frying again. Then add the blended tomatoes, some salt and pepper and dried ground chilli and simmer over low heat for about 15 minutes or until you have a nice loose sauce, not too thick. Add the cream and let it bubble up for a moment. Then keep warm while you make the gnocchi.

To make the gnocchi, cook the potatoes in their skins in boiling salted water until soft. Remove and drain. Cool a little, then peel. Pass the warm potato through a potato ricer. Mix in as much of your flour as necessary to make a very soft dough — the less flour you have to use, the better and softer your gnocchi will be. Cut chunks of the mixture off and gently roll out logs about 2 cm (¾ inch) thick, without pressing down too hard. Cut into pieces about 2.5 cm (1 inch) long.

Meanwhile, melt the butter in a small saucepan over the highest heat until it starts fizzing. Add the scampi pieces and cook until they are golden on the bottom, all the liquid has evaporated and the scampi are once again frying in the butter and there are some crusty bits here and there. Add a little salt and when the scampi are golden in places and the flesh is bright white and soft, add the Cognac and flame the pan, standing back so you don't burn yourself. Add the scampi to the tomato sauce.

Bring a large pot of salted water to the boil. Add half the gnocchi to the boiling water and cook until they bob up to the surface, then lift out with a slotted spoon and add to the hot tomato sauce while you cook the second batch. Once the gnocchi have all been added to the tomato sauce, increase the heat to high and add about 4 tablespoons of the gnocchi cooking water to loosen things up a bit. Fold everything together.

Allow the sauce to bubble away and toss the pan by flicking your wrist, to coat everything rather than stabbing at the gnocchi with a spoon to mix together. Serve up at once into flat bowls or plates with chopped parsley and a grinding of black pepper.

SERVES 4 (ABUNDANTLY)
OR 6 (SCANTILY)

9–10 scampi (langoustines, red-claw crayfish or large prawns/shrimp) — you need about 150 g (5½ oz) of scampi meat

1 tablespoon butter

1 tablespoon Cognac or brandy

1 tablespoon chopped flat-leaf parsley

**TOMATO SAUCE**

600 g (1 lb 5 oz) tinned peeled tomatoes

60 ml (2 fl oz/¼ cup) olive oil

½ white onion, finely chopped

2 garlic cloves, chopped

60 ml (2 fl oz/¼ cup) white wine

a pinch of dried ground chilli

1 tablespoon cream

**GNOCCHI**

650 g (1 lb 7 oz) floury potatoes, washed but unpeeled

about 150 g (5½ oz) plain (all-purpose) flour, less if possible

# VEGETABLE RISOTTO

The winning stroke here is the fried artichokes on top. The combination of the artichokes and fresh mint to pull through the risotto as you are eating is truly great. When you are making your vegetable broth, be sure to add the trimmings from the asparagus to give a depth of flavour.

Trim the asparagus and slice on the diagonal, leaving the tips whole. Add the trimmings to your vegetable broth as it simmers.

To prepare your artichokes, trim away the outer leaves and cut a slice off the top. Halve the artichoke and remove the hairy choke if it has one, then cut each half into fine slices 4–5 mm (¼ inch) thick. (Keep them covered with cold water and a little lemon juice to prevent them turning black.)

Heat the olive oil in a wide pot and sauté the onion until well softened. Add the asparagus, zucchini and peas and sauté on high heat for a moment to just take the flavours. Add the rice, turning it through so it is well coated with oil. Season with salt and pepper, then add the wine and let that bubble away. Add 500 ml (17 fl oz/2 cups) of hot broth, lower the heat and simmer for about 10 minutes until much of the broth has been absorbed. Add another cupful of hot broth, stir in gently and then leave it to do its thing, adding another cupful of broth when necessary until the rice is tender and creamy (about 20 minutes in total). Don't let it get so dry that you have to keep stirring.

Remove from the heat, then add the butter, parmesan and parsley and stir gently through to combine. Add salt if needed.

Just before your risotto is ready, drain the artichokes, pat dry and pat lightly in flour on both sides. Use a non-stick pan that will fit the artichokes in one layer if possible. Just cover the bottom with the light olive oil and heat up. Add the artichokes and fry until golden and crisp on both sides. Lift out onto a plate lined with paper towel to drain. Serve the risotto with a heap of hot fried artichokes on top, plus the fresh mint, extra parmesan and black pepper.

**SERVES 4**

225 g (8 oz) asparagus

1.25 litres (44 fl oz/5 cups) hot vegetable broth (see page 136)

2 artichokes

juice of ½ a lemon

80 ml (2½ fl oz/⅓ cup) olive oil

1 small white onion, chopped

200 g (7 oz) zucchini (courgettes), sliced

150 g (5½ oz) fresh or frozen peas

250 g (9 oz) risotto rice

125 ml (4 fl oz/½ cup) white wine

30 g (1 oz) butter

3–4 tablespoons grated parmesan cheese, plus extra to serve

2 tablespoons chopped flat-leaf parsley

plain (all-purpose) flour, for coating

light olive oil

a handful of mint sprigs

# PRAWN & SPINACH BROWN RICE RISOTTO

This is a very adaptable recipe with ingredients that can be easily swapped for others if you prefer. You can also make it with white rice: just add your broth as instructed and follow the same method, but the cooking time will be much shorter (about twenty minutes).

SERVES 3–4

Peel and devein the prawns (keeping the shells), leaving the tails on four of them, if you like. Butterfly these four and chop up the rest. Put the butterflied prawns in one side of a bowl, the chopped prawns in the other side, then cover the bowl and keep it in the fridge.

Put the prawn shells and half the oil into a pan and cook over a high heat for about a minute, stirring a few times, until the shells turn pink. Add the garlic and, when you can smell it, add the passata. Sauté for a few more minutes. Add 1.25 litres (44 fl oz/5 cups) of hot water, the parsley stalks and lemon slices. Season with salt and pepper and bring to the boil. Simmer for about 20 minutes, then strain into a clean pan and keep warm over very low heat.

Heat the butter and the remaining oil in a heavy-based pan suitable for making risotto. Add the shallots and sauté for a few minutes over medium heat until lightly golden and softened, then add the rice. Stir and turn it for a few minutes so that it is well coated. Add a ladleful of the broth and stir with a wooden spoon until the liquid has been absorbed. Reduce the heat to low, add another ladleful of broth and stir until it has been absorbed. Carry on like this for about 40 minutes, then add the chopped prawns, chopped parsley and spinach. Continue cooking in the same way for another 10 minutes or so, until the rice is tender but still a little bit firm in the centre. If you run out of broth before this time, just carry on with hot water. Add the extra butter, sit the whole prawns on top of the rice and cook for a few minutes more until the prawns are pink. Sprinkle a little salt over the prawns, put a cloth over the rice, remove from the heat and leave to stand for 10 minutes before serving.

8 raw prawns (shrimp)

80 ml (2½ fl oz/⅓ cup) olive oil

2 garlic cloves, finely chopped

250 ml (9 fl oz/1 cup) tomato passata (puréed tomatoes)

4 flat-leaf parsley stalks, plus 1 tablespoon chopped parsley leaves

2 lemon slices

20 g (¾ oz) butter, plus 30 g (1 oz) extra

2 French shallots, finely chopped

300 g (10½ oz/1½ cups) brown rice

100 g (3½ oz) English spinach leaves, chopped

# RISOTTO WITH FRIED EGG

These are all the things my family loves — white risotto, egg, parmesan — on one plate. The egg yolk must be soft when you serve it so that it can drip into the rice, and we like the white to be golden and frayed around the edge.

**SERVES 4**

Heat half the butter and 2 tablespoons of oil in a heavy-based pan suitable for making risotto. Sauté the shallots over low heat until light gold and then stir in the rice with a wooden spoon. Stir for a few minutes to completely coat the rice and let it cook just a bit. Add the wine and when that has evaporated, add all of the broth. Add a few good gratings of nutmeg and taste for salt (your broth will probably be seasoned enough). Simmer uncovered over high heat for about 15 minutes, or until the rice has absorbed much of the liquid. If it seems as if it needs a bit more liquid, add some hot water. Remove from the heat and stir in the remaining butter and the parmesan. Taste for salt, adjusting if necessary. Leave with the lid on so that the steam continues to cook the rice.

Heat the remaining oil in a large non-stick frying pan and briefly fry the sage leaves until crisp. Remove with tongs. Gently break the eggs into the pan and sprinkle a little salt on the yolks. Cook until the edges of the white are a bit golden. Cover the pan with a lid and fry until the yolks are just slightly opaque on the surface but still soft inside (they are best when the undersides are golden and a bit crisp).

Scoop the rice onto serving plates and top each serving with an egg and a couple of sage leaves, being careful not to break the yolk just yet. Serve with a sprinkling of parmesan and a few grinds of black pepper for those who want it.

40 g (1½ oz) butter

60 ml (2 fl oz/¼ cup) olive oil

2 French shallots, chopped

320 g (11¼ oz) risotto rice

125 ml (4 fl oz/½ cup) white wine

1 litre (35 fl oz/4 cups) hot vegetable broth

freshly grated nutmeg

40 g (1½ oz) grated parmesan cheese, plus extra to serve

about 8 fresh sage leaves

4 eggs, at room temperature

# ASPARAGUS & SCAMPI RISOTTO

This is also good and delicate with just scampi or just asparagus. Some people don't serve parmesan with seafood, but I put a bit in here.

SERVES 4

12–16 scampi (langoustines, red-claw crayfish or large prawns/shrimp)

**BROTH**
1 large carrot
½ onion
1 bay leaf
a few peppercorns

360 g (12¾ oz) asparagus
½ onion, finely chopped
80 ml (2½ fl oz/⅓ cup) olive oil
250 g (9 oz) risotto rice
125 ml (4 fl oz/½ cup) white wine
1 tablespoon Cognac
1 tablespoon butter
2 tablespoons grated parmesan cheese

To make the broth, peel and clean the scampi and halve them down the middle. Set the meat aside for now, but rinse the heads and shells and put them in a pot with 1.5 litres (52 fl oz/6 cups) of water, the carrot, onion, bay leaf, peppercorns and some salt. Bring to the boil, then simmer for 30 minutes, then strain and keep the broth hot.

Discard the woody ends from the asparagus and cut off the tips. Keep the tips on one side and chop the stems. Sauté the onion in 3 tablespoons of the olive oil until well softened, add the chopped asparagus and sauté briefly.

Add the rice, turning it through so it is well coated with oil. Add the white wine and let it bubble up until much of it has evaporated. Add 500 ml (17 fl oz/2 cups) of the broth, stir well and simmer for 10–15 minutes or until it has almost all been absorbed. Add another 2 cupfuls of broth, stir and cook for another 5–10 minutes. Add another ½ cup of broth if you need it for a creamy risotto.

When your risotto is almost ready, heat the remaining oil in a small pan, add the scampi and asparagus tips and cook over high heat for 2 minutes, turning the scampi over when they have a pale golden crust underneath. Add the Cognac, stand back and flame the pan. Add a bit of salt and toss it all together, then take off the heat.

Stir the butter and parmesan into the risotto, then tip the scampi and asparagus tips into the risotto. Add salt if needed, quickly toss it all through and serve at once with black pepper.

# MUSSEL RICE

This is often made with all the shells removed, so if you prefer you can make it that way too (I love the shells). This is a dish from northern Greece, which is best served warm just after you have made it. It is great alone, or along with other fish plates as part of a meze. Choose lovely fresh mussels. Nice with ouzo on ice.

SERVES 4–6

De-beard the mussels and scrub them clean with a wire brush under running water. Drain. Give each one a tap and discard those that stay open. Heat 2 tablespoons of the oil in a high-sided pot large enough to hold all the mussels. Add the whole garlic and when it starts to smell good, add the drained mussels, parsley and wine. Put over high heat and cook, covered, until the mussels have opened. Remove the opened ones and give the others another chance. Remove from the heat and strain, keeping the liquid. Now discard any mussels that have not opened. When cool enough to handle remove half of the mussels from their shells. Discard the empty shells and put the mussels together with the other ones still in their shells. Keep aside for now.

Heat the rest of the oil in a wide non-stick pot. Add the spring onion and sauté over a low heat until soft and golden. Stir in the chopped garlic and half the dill and when they smell good, add the ouzo. Cook until it evaporates, then add the tomato. Increase the heat to medium and simmer for a few minutes, then add the rice, turning it through to coat well. Make the mussel broth up to 1 litre (35 fl oz /4 cups) with hot water and add this to the pot with a little salt. Bring to the boil, lower the heat and simmer for about 10–12 minutes or until a lot of the liquid has been absorbed. Taste, adding salt if necessary.

Add all the mussels, shelled and unshelled, turn through with a wooden spoon and simmer for another 5 minutes, checking that nothing sticks to the bottom of the pot. Remove from the heat, add the remaining dill and fluff up the rice. Cover the pot with a clean tea towel. Put the lid back on and leave it for another 10 minutes or so to steam and finish cooking. Serve with a grind of pepper and a scattering of the extra dill.

1.5 kg (3 lb 5 oz) black mussels, not too big

120 ml (4 fl oz) olive oil

3 garlic cloves, peeled, 1 left whole and 2 chopped

2 thick flat-leaf parsley stalks with leaves

125 ml (4 fl oz/½ cup) white wine

180 g (6½ oz) round spring onions (scallions), chopped with some green also

4 tablespoons coarsely chopped dill, plus extra, chopped, for serving

60 ml (2 fl oz/¼ cup) ouzo

2 tomatoes, grated on the large holes of a grater (so that the skin stays behind in your hand)

400 g (14 oz) medium-grain rice

# 6

# ~ SEAFOOD ~

# POLENTA-CRUSTED ANCHOVIES

The size of anchovies varies greatly and this is also lovely if you can get small sardines (the preparation is the same). These are pressed in polenta, fried and then dressed with an onion, olive oil and lemon dressing. You can easily make a larger quantity if you like … they keep well in the fridge for a day or so and even stay crisp on account of the polenta.

SERVES 4–6

Put the onion in a bowl. Cover with cold water and the vinegar, leave for an hour or so, then rinse, drain and pat dry.

To fillet the anchovies, cut off the heads, then make a slit down the side of each fish and remove the guts and bones. Open out each anchovy flat, hinged like a book with the tail on. Rinse and pat dry very well with paper towel.

Pat the anchovy fillets in the polenta while your oil is heating in a non-stick frying pan. Fry the anchovies in a single layer (or in two batches, depending on the size of your pan) until golden and crisp on both sides. Remove to a plate lined with paper towel.

In a compact bowl, make a layer of anchovies with some onion and parsley. Make another layer of anchovies, onion and parsley on top.

Mix the lemon juice and extra virgin olive oil to make a dressing and drizzle over the top so that it falls between the fish. Season with salt and pepper. Serve straight away or cover and leave to absorb the flavours. This will keep in the fridge for a day or so (after which you could add a bit more dressing if you liked).

1 small red onion, finely sliced

3 tablespoons red wine vinegar

200 g (7 oz) fresh anchovies (about 12–15)

about 4 tablespoons polenta

olive oil, for frying

1½ tablespoons chopped flat-leaf parsley

**DRESSING**
juice of ½ a lemon

3 tablespoons extra virgin olive oil

# CALAMARI WITH BUTTER, LEMON & GARLIC

This must be cooked in a really hot chargrill pan and then combined with the sauce to serve. You could also add a little chilli here if you like. Serve with white rice or pasta, or just bread to wipe up the buttery garlic.

To clean the calamari, pull the tentacles away from the body. Remove the transparent quill from inside the body and rinse the body well under cold running water. Holding the tentacles firmly with one hand, squeeze out the little beak and cut it away, leaving the tentacles whole. Rinse the tentacles. Cut the body into rings about 3 cm (1¼ inches) thick, leaving the tentacles whole (if they seem particularly large, cut them in half). Pat dry.

Heat the butter in a saucepan and, when it sizzles, add the lemon juice. Season with salt and pepper. Add the garlic and let it sizzle for a moment to flavour the butter but not burn. Stir in the parsley and remove from the heat.

Heat a ridged chargrill pan (griddle) to very hot (it should be just about smoking). Scatter with about half the calamari in a single layer (you will have to do it in two batches) and cook it over the highest possible heat. When you see that the calamari has darkened in parts on the underside, turn over with tongs and cook until the other side has darkened (take care that it doesn't burn though, or it will taste bitter). Move it around in the pan with a wooden spoon and let it cook for a couple of minutes more, then add it to the warm butter in the saucepan while you cook the next batch. Season to taste if necessary and serve hot, directly from the pan, with lemon wedges.

**SERVES 4–6 AS AN APPETISER OR 3–4 AS A LIGHT MEAL**

1 kg (2 lb 4 oz) calamari (preferably baby calamari)
100 g (3½ oz) butter
juice of 1½ lemons
3 garlic cloves, finely chopped
2 tablespoons chopped flat-leaf parsley
lemon wedges, to serve

# SARDINES IN ESCABECHE

These are quick to make and keep well in the fridge for a day or so. The Portuguese will often use smaller sardines for a dish like this, while the larger plumper catch are saved for the charcoal grill. These are lovely with bread at room temperature, or even cold when they've been sitting for a while and have soaked up the flavours. If you prefer, you can fillet the fish first (it's not such a hectic job), so you don't have to fiddle with the bones on your plate.

**SERVES 2–3**

Rinse the sardines and pat dry. Pat well in the cornflour to coat on both sides. Heat the oil in a small non-stick frying pan that will hold the sardines in a single layer without being too tightly packed. Fry the fish until deep golden and crusty on both sides. Drain on paper towel and put into a dish where they fit snugly in a single layer.

Heat 2 tablespoons of olive oil in a small pan and sauté the onion for a minute or so. Add the carrot and cook until just slightly softened. Add the garlic and, when you start to smell it, add the tomato paste. Stir well, then add the vinegar and port. Bubble up for 5 minutes or so until it thickens, add 125 ml (4 fl oz/½ cup) of water and carry on cooking for another few minutes until you have a good sauce.

Pour over the fried sardines so that they are covered, then scatter with some coarse salt and pepper. Sprinkle with the parsley just before serving, either warm or cold.

6–8 sardines (about 250 g/9 oz), cleaned and gutted

cornflour (cornstarch)

olive oil, for frying

1 small onion, sliced into rings

1 carrot, peeled and thinly sliced on the diagonal

1 garlic clove, chopped

1 teaspoon tomato paste (concentrated purée)

125 ml (4 fl oz/½ cup) white wine vinegar

1 tablespoon ruby port

1 tablespoon chopped flat-leaf parsley

# PRAWNS IN BEER

A couple of tablespoons of cream bubbled in at the end is very good.
Or you could take it in an entirely different direction with a squeeze
of lemon and a handful of chopped coriander (cilantro) or parsley.

SERVES 4–6

Leave the shells on the prawns but cut down the back of each one and devein
so they take in the flavour of the sauce. Rinse well. Heat half the butter in a
deep frying pan. When it sizzles, add a layer of prawns, pressing them down
well so they are butterflied and become golden brown and crisp. If there isn't
room for them all in your pan, remove them as they're cooked to make space
for the rest. Don't overcook them or they'll lose their succulence.

When all the prawns are cooked, add the paprika, piri piri, salt and some
black pepper to the pan. Cook for a bit, then add the garlic and the rest of the
butter. When you can smell the garlic, remove the prawns to a plate.

Pour the beer into the pan and increase the heat to high so that it bubbles
and thickens. Return the prawns to the pan.

Put the lid on and rock the pan from side to side to coat the prawns with
hot sauce. Serve with crusty bread or chips to dip in the sauce. And a glass
of cold beer …

1 kg (2 lb 4 oz) large raw prawns
  (shrimp)
100 g (3½ oz) butter
½ teaspoon sweet paprika
a pinch of ground piri piri
1 teaspoon coarse salt
4 garlic cloves, roughly chopped
185 ml (6 fl oz/¾ cup) beer

# FRIED CALAMARI

Please use lovely fresh and tender calamari here. It must be eaten with just a scattering of salt, pepper and oregano, and some lemon on the side for whoever would like. Have a bowl of plain flour and a bowl of water ready and your pan of oil heating up. Sometimes calamari splatters and pops in the pan, so it's a good idea to have a splatter mat that you can cover the pan with while the calamari are frying.

Cut the heads off and pull the innards from the calamari. Pull the transparent quill out of the body. Cut off the tentacles just above the eyes. Rinse the bodies and tentacles in cold water and dry them on paper towel. Slice the bodies into rings of about 1.5 cm (⅝ inch) or as you like them. Keep the tentacles whole (unless they are big).

Put the flour on a deep plate, and pour cold water into a deep bowl. Pour olive oil to a depth of at least 1 cm (½ inch) into a frying pan and put over a high heat. Pat the calamari in the flour to coat well, shake off the excess then quickly dip them in the cold water. Pat them again well in the flour and shake off lightly. Fry in batches in the hot oil, turning them once, until they are golden and crusty. Remove to a plate lined with paper towel to drain while frying the rest. Mix together the salt, pepper and oregano then scatter it over the lot and serve at once with lemon for those who would like it.

SERVES 2

400 g (14 oz) small–medium calamari
plain (all-purpose) flour, for dusting
light olive oil, for frying
1 teaspoon salt
few grinds of black pepper
2 teaspoons dried oregano
lemon quarters, to serve

# HERRINGS MARINATED IN VINEGAR WITH DILL & ALLSPICE

This is how my Finnish mother makes her herrings. There are many ways to marinate and serve herrings and these are my favourite, marinated in vinegar, some sugar, carrots, onions, dill and allspice. I also like them done with tomato and onion. They need to stay in their marinade for about three days before you eat them. Keep the jar in the fridge and make sure that the herrings are immersed in the liquid. They will keep for about a week in the fridge and the flavour will get stronger. I use lightly smoked salted herrings but you can use unsmoked if you prefer. You might also like to add a dried red chilli to your jar. These herrings are good served with rye bread and room temperature potatoes that have been boiled with salt and dill stalks. Rinse the herrings and soak them overnight in cold water, changing it a couple of times.

To fillet a herring, cut off the head and tail and then open the fish out flat, skin side up. Using your thumb, press down firmly along the backbone. This will nearly release the bones from the flesh. Turn the fish over and use scissors to snip through the backbone at the head and tail. Pull away the backbone, working towards the tail end. Remove any stray bones with your fingers or tweezers. Wash the fish and pat it dry. Cut the herring fillets into 2–3 cm (1¼ inch) strips.

Meanwhile, boil the vinegar, sugar, peppercorns and 250 ml (9 fl oz/1 cup) water in a small pan for a few minutes, stirring to make sure the sugar has dissolved. Remove from the heat and add the allspice and bay leaves. Leave to cool down completely.

Layer the herring strips in jars with the dill, onion rings and carrots. Pour the cooled liquid into the jars, put on the lids tightly and keep refrigerated. Marinate for three days (or at least 24 hours if you're in a hurry) before serving. The herrings are also good drained of vinegar and served on a plate with a drizzle of extra virgin olive oil.

**SERVES 4**

4 lightly smoked salted herrings (about 1 kg/2 lb 4 oz), gutted

500 ml (17 fl oz/2 cups) light red wine vinegar

about 120 g (4¼ oz) sugar

1 teaspoon whole peppercorns

1 flat teaspoon whole allspice (pimento) berries

3 bay leaves

a small handful of dill or wild fennel sprigs, roughly chopped

3 onions, sliced into rings

2 largish carrots, sliced

# RED MULLET
# WITH TOMATOES

This is also good served at room temperature. It doesn't need much else to accompany it as a main course; just bread or maybe some boiled potatoes and a salad. You can use capers in vinegar (just drain them first), or the salted ones, rinsed.

SERVES 4

Put the olive oil and garlic in a large saucepan over medium heat. When you can smell the garlic, add the tomatoes and a little salt and cook for about 10 minutes until the tomatoes have melted, adding 125 ml (4 fl oz/½ cup) of hot water towards the end of this time. Stir in the capers, olives and parsley.

Meanwhile, sprinkle the flour onto a flat plate. Lightly pat the fish fillets in the flour, season with a little salt and add to the tomato. Cook for about 8 minutes, turning them over once, until they are cooked. Check the seasoning and serve with black pepper and some bread.

3 tablespoons olive oil

1 garlic clove, lightly crushed with the flat of a knife

400 g (14 oz) tinned chopped tomatoes

2 tablespoons capers

60 g (2¼ oz/¼ cup) pitted green olives, chopped

2 tablespoons chopped flat-leaf parsley

30 g (1 oz) plain (all-purpose) flour

8 red mullet fillets (about 30 g/1 oz each), all bones removed but skin left on

# CLAMS & TOMATO

This is how my lovely sister-in-law, Luisa (half-Venetian, half-Tuscan), likes to make clams. She adds a dash of cream to the tomato sauce, which makes it beautifully sweet and mellow. These can be served with bread or are great tossed into pasta with a little of the pasta cooking water to loosen things up. Try penne, spaghetti or any pasta you like: you'll need about 280 g (10 oz). You can also add a handful of chopped herbs to the sauce if you like. I have used *vongole veraci* (carpet shell clams) here but any clams are fine. Your clams will probably have been purged of sand already but check with the fishmonger, otherwise you'll need to soak them for a day in a colander standing in well-salted water, changing the water several times.

To make the tomato sauce, heat the oil in a frying pan and cook the onion over low heat until it almost disappears and is very soft (it should not be dark but should be very well cooked). Add the passata, a grinding of salt and pepper and a good pinch of crushed dried chilli. Simmer uncovered for 10–15 minutes until it all thickens into a lovely sauce. Add the cream and allow the sauce to bubble for a couple of minutes more. Take the pan off the heat.

If you've been soaking your clams, give them a good swirl in the water, rinse them, drain and leave in the colander. Heat the oil with the garlic in a large frying pan (that has a lid). Once you start to smell the garlic, add the clams and wine. Turn the heat up to the maximum and put the lid on the pan. Let the clams all steam open. Discard any that refuse to open.

Take the clams out of the pan. Check for sand by pressing on the bottom of the pan with the back of a spoon. If you think there might be sand, then strain the sauce through a colander lined with muslin.

Add all the clam cooking liquid to the tomato sauce and simmer for 5–10 minutes until the flavours have merged and the liquid has reduced a little. You want there to be quite a lot of liquid but it shouldn't be too watery. Return the clams to the pan and heat through for a minute. Serve straight from the pan with bread.

**SERVES 4**

**TOMATO SAUCE**
4 tablespoons olive oil
½ small onion, very finely chopped
375 ml (13 fl oz/1½ cups) passata (puréed tomatoes)
a good pinch of crushed dried chilli
2 tablespoons cream

**CLAMS**
3 tablespoons olive oil
2 garlic cloves, chopped
1 kg (2 lb 4 oz) clams in their shells
125 ml (4 fl oz/½ cup) white wine

# SALMON CEVICHE WITH CORIANDER, CHILLI & LIME

This is a wonderful dish of my friend Ana's that, thank goodness, has managed to grace our table many times. If you love every single ingredient that goes into something, how can you not love the finished dish? Changing quantities here is very simple: just add more of anything you like. You could also add a little olive oil if you are not using an oily fish such as salmon. Ana says ceviche is often eaten in Peru, using all kinds of fish: you can try prawns (shrimp), squid, mussels, oysters and just about any other fish fillet. This could be served with some firm green leaves and sliced red onions as a salad or with boiled potatoes. It would serve six as an antipasto or four as a salad or light main meal. Ceviche should be prepared at least four hours before you want to eat, to allow the flavours to mingle well and for the fish to 'cook' in the lime juice. It is even good the next day.

**SERVES 4–6**

Remove any bones from the salmon (you can check for bones by stroking the salmon up and down). Slice it into pieces about 1 cm (½ inch) thick and put in a wide, non-metallic bowl.

Mix the lime juice, chilli, coriander, cumin and garlic together then pour over the fish and season with salt and pepper. Take the grated ginger between your fingers and firmly squeeze the juice over the salmon (discard the pulp that's left). Mix through gently, cover with plastic wrap and refrigerate for at least 4 hours before serving.

600 g (1 lb 5 oz) salmon fillet, all skin removed

juice of 4 limes

2–3 red chillies, seeded and finely chopped

2 tablespoons chopped coriander (cilantro)

¼ teaspoon ground cumin

2 garlic cloves, very finely chopped

4 cm (1½ inch) piece of ginger, peeled and grated

# SALT COD WITH TOMATOES, PEPPERS & OLIVES

Before you use the salt cod you need to soak it to remove the excess salt. Rinse the cod pieces first, then put them in a large bowl with enough water to completely immerse them. Cover the bowl and refrigerate, changing the water three or four times a day. Ask your fishmonger how long you need to soak the cod (it's usually about two to three days). If you're unsure, test the cod by breaking off a small fleck and tasting it. The tail part is always a bit more salty. In some places you can buy ready-soaked salt cod, which is very reliable and convenient. You could also make this with fresh cod or other fish fillets (without the soaking, of course).

SERVES 2

Preheat the oven to 200°C (400°F/Gas 6). Drain the salt cod well, pat dry with paper towel and cut into three or four pieces.

Heat 2 tablespoons of the oil in a frying pan and sauté the onion until softened and turning golden. Add the pepper and cook until golden. Add the garlic and bay leaf and turn through the oil, then add the wine and let it bubble up. Add the tomatoes with about 3 tablespoons of water. Simmer for a few minutes and remove from the heat. Check the seasoning, as you may not need extra salt because of the cod. Scrape the tomato sauce into an oven dish that will fit the salt cod snugly in a single layer.

Cut the potatoes in half vertically so they are round, or into quarters if they're quite big. Lay the cod over the tomato sauce in a single layer with the potato pieces dotted here and there. Some of the sauce will find its way over the fish and potatoes. Drizzle the rest of the oil over the top. Cover the dish with foil and put in the oven. Bake for about 20 minutes, then take off the foil and cook for another 30 minutes or until the fish and potatoes are cooked and the tomatoes and onions are turning crusty golden here and there. Scatter with olives and cook for another 5 minutes. Sprinkle with parsley to serve, if you like.

about 350 g (12 oz) salt cod, soaked

5 tablespoons olive oil

1 onion, halved and thinly sliced

½ red pepper (capsicum), seeded and roughly chopped

1 garlic clove, chopped

1 bay leaf

3 tablespoons white wine

200 g (7 oz) tinned chopped tomatoes

6 small new potatoes, peeled

about 10 olives

# PRAWNS WITH LEMON, PIRI PIRI, GARLIC & FETA

This is amazing. Everyone who has tasted this dish loves it and still now I use it for a special occasion dinner — it seems very 'celebration'. My mother still salts every single prawn individually; once she has slit and removed the dark line of the prawn she sprinkles salt along this. You can just scatter salt over each layer in the saucepan. My mother always uses piri piri, which is a wonderfully flavoured full-potency chilli that we get in South Africa. Substitute your favourite chilli powder or cayenne pepper, using as much as you like. I like a good balance of strong flavours but the chilli should not be too overpowering. You can clean the prawns beforehand and keep them covered in a colander in the fridge, then you'll only need about 20 minutes before serving. This dish needs very little else — bread, some white rice or couscous and a large green salad.

**SERVES 6 OR MORE**

2 kg (4 lb 8 oz) large raw prawns
   (shrimp), unpeeled

200 g (7 oz) butter

10 garlic cloves, finely chopped

45 g (1½ oz/¾ cup) chopped
   flat-leaf parsley

less than 1 teaspoon piri piri spice
   or chilli powder

juice of 4 lemons

400 g (14 oz) feta cheese

Clean the prawns and cut a slit through the shell down the back from the bottom of the head to the beginning of the tail. Remove the dark vein with the point of a sharp knife. Rinse the prawns under running water and drain well.

Dot about 80 g (2¾ oz) of the butter over the base of a large cast-iron casserole dish. Arrange a single layer of prawns in the dish and season with salt. Scatter about a third of the garlic and parsley over the top. Sprinkle with a little of the piri piri.

Dot about half of the remaining butter over the top and arrange another layer of prawns, scattered with garlic, parsley and piri piri. Repeat the layer, finishing up the ingredients. Put the lid on, turn the heat to medium–high and cook for about 10 minutes, until the prawns have brightened up a lot and their flesh is white. Add the lemon juice, crumble the feta over the top and rock the dish from side to side to move the sauce about. Spoon some sauce over the prawns. Cover the casserole, lower the heat and cook for another 10 minutes or until the feta has just melted, shaking the pan again. Take the dish straight to the table and give everyone a finger bowl with hot water and lemon juice to clean their hands afterwards.

# PAN-FRIED FISH WITH VINEGAR

My friend Corinne taught me this dish and it's a beauty. It's quick but a bit delicate to make — you need to have your fish cooked just right and simultaneously make sure that nothing burns. So get everything ready before you start. You need nice round, plumpish baby fish here. I used bream here, but use anything that will fit in your pan — snapper, flathead, bass, mackerel, haddock … Ask your fishmonger to gut, scale and trim away the fins.

Pat the fish dry, salt well, then pat in flour on both sides. Heat the oil in a frying pan large enough to hold both fish. When hot, add the fish and cook for a few minutes over high heat until golden underneath. Turn over and salt.

Add the garlic and bay leaves and throw in almost half the rosemary. Cook again until the fish is golden underneath. Turn over carefully, taking care not to break the fish, and salt the new topside. The heat should still be high, so sit the garlic and bay on top of the fish if necessary. Add the vinegar and let it bubble for 5 minutes or so until thickened a little. Add the rest of the rosemary and some black pepper and spoon the liquid over the fish a few times. There should be lots of sauce for serving and the fish will be cooked through.

Take the whole pan to the table (with a plate for the bones). The rosemary garlic oil is delicious scraped from the bottom of the pan with chips or bread.

**SERVES 2**

2 baby fish (each about 300 g/ 10 ½ oz), cleaned, gutted and scaled

coarse salt

a little plain (all-purpose) flour

125 ml (4 fl oz/½ cup) olive oil

2 garlic cloves, peeled and squashed a bit

2 bay leaves

2½ tablespoons chopped rosemary leaves

125 ml (4 fl oz/½ cup) white wine vinegar

# GRILLED SQUID WITH CHOURIÇO & LEMON CORIANDER OIL

This is a beauty. Sometimes I have bought frozen, cleaned baby squid tubes with tentacles attached — they certainly save preparation time.

While in Portugal, I ate grilled squid in many places, the first time in a restaurant on the north coast. I pointed to table three, indicating that I wanted some of the sauce they had. But they are having meat, she mimed. I pantomimed that I'd like to try it anyway and it was fantastic. I had some grilled *chouriço* on the table and I ate them together. In true Portuguese style I left the restaurant after a chat in a non-existent common language with the ladies in the kitchen, holding a small glass bottle full of lovely coriander sauce.

---

If you're using wooden skewers, soak them in water for a while first so they don't scorch. To prepare the squid, firmly pull the head and innards from the body and wash the body well. Cut off the head just below the eyes, leaving the tentacles in one piece, and discard the head. Pull out the transparent quill, rinse the tube and peel off the outer membrane.

Cut the *chouriço* into about 8 chunks. Thread the pieces of squid (body and tentacles) and *chouriço* alternately onto your skewers.

Heat the butter and garlic in a small pan. Sizzle just until the garlic chunks are starting to crisp up but are not yet turning golden. Remove from the heat immediately as the garlic will carry on simmering in the butter as it cools.

To make the lemon coriander oil, pulse half the coriander with the lemon juice, oil, salt and anchovies in a blender until you have chunky flecks of green sauce.

Preheat your grill. Brush the skewers with the garlic butter and grill until charred here and there (probably more noticeable on the *chouriço*), brushing occasionally with the butter. Take great care not to overcook — the squid must be cooked through but still tender. Serve the skewers drizzled with the lemon coriander oil. Lovely with boiled potatoes dressed with olive oil.

**SERVES 2 (OR 4 AS A STARTER)**

600 g (1 lb 5 oz) baby squid
150 g (5½ oz) *chouriço* sausage
2 tablespoons butter
2 garlic cloves, roughly chopped

**LEMON CORIANDER OIL**
a handful of coriander (cilantro) leaves
juice of ½ a lemon
2 tablespoons olive oil
½ teaspoon salt
2 large anchovy fillets packed in oil, drained

# FISH CAKES

These are complete on their own with a squeeze of lemon juice and a side salad, but wonderful with chips and some homemade mayonnaise. Small helpers might enjoy squishing the mixture into patties with their hands — my daughter loved this part and wasn't at all worried about the fish and potato flecks that were taking off out of the bowl.

MAKES 12–15

Put a pan of water on to boil and add the carrot, celery, lemon, peppercorns, half the parsley stalks and the salt. Simmer over medium–low heat for about 10 minutes, then add all the fish. Simmer for 10–15 minutes until the fish is soft, but not collapsing, and flakes easily. Turn off the heat and leave the fish to cool in the broth. Drain and flake the fish into a bowl, removing any little bones as you go.

Meanwhile, simmer the potatoes and the rest of the parsley stalks in salted water for 15 minutes or so until the potatoes are soft. Drain and mash.

Heat a dash of the olive oil in a non-stick frying pan and sauté the spring onions until soft and slightly golden. Mash the fish with a potato masher and then add the potatoes. Squish the mixture through your fingers, like playing with sand on a beach, and pick out any bones or skin that you might have previously missed.

Whip the eggs and remaining olive oil in a small bowl and then add to the fish mixture with the paprika, chopped parsley and spring onion. Mix through well, still with your hands. Add salt or pepper, if needed. Form the mixture into balls about the size of an egg, then flatten slightly into patties. Put the breadcrumbs on a plate and pat the fish cakes into them, coating them all over. Put the fish cakes on a tray, cover with plastic wrap and chill for an hour.

Heat 2–3 cm (about 1 inch) of oil in a large non-stick frying pan. Fry the fish cakes in batches, turning them gently with a spatula until they are golden on both sides. Lift them out onto a plate lined with paper towel to absorb the excess oil.

Serve warm with lemon wedges and a little extra salt, if you like. Leftovers can be pressed into sandwiches with some shredded lettuce and mayonnaise.

1 small carrot, peeled and halved

a small piece of leafy celery stalk

1 slice of lemon, 1.5 cm (⅝ inch) thick

4 peppercorns

a handful of flat-leaf parsley stalks

1 teaspoon salt

270 g (9½ oz) mixed boneless white fish fillets (such as bass, cod or other firm white fish)

100 g (3½ oz) boneless salmon fillet

625 g (1 lb 6 oz) potatoes, peeled and chopped

1 tablespoon olive oil

2 tablespoons diced spring onions (scallions)

2 eggs

1 teaspoon sweet paprika

3 tablespoons chopped flat-leaf parsley

light olive oil, for frying

about 85 g (3 oz) dry breadcrumbs

lemon wedges, to serve

# FISH GRILL WITH LEMON

This is one of my favourites — a real Portuguese feast. It sums up everything about the Portuguese table to me. Try to get some good variety in taste and form … a thick fish fillet, a plump fish that you can butterfly and grill opened, some big sardines, even a few clams as I had them in Portugal, simply set on the grill until they opened. A couple of mackerel are also a beauty here. Do as the Portuguese do and use whatever fish are freshest and best on the day. Have your fish all cleaned, gutted, scaled (and fins cut away with scissors) and ready for the barbecue (the fishmonger can do this for you). Your clams will probably have been purged of sand already but check with your fishmonger, otherwise you'll need to soak them for a day in a colander standing in a bowl of well-salted water, changing the water several times. Have your side dishes ready before you put the fish on the grill, and the wine cold, and some fado playing …

First make the lemon oil: heat the butter with the garlic, paprika and piri piri until you start to smell the garlic. Remove from the heat and stir in the tomato paste, oil and lemon juice. Season well, add the parsley, cover and set aside.

Have all your serving plates ready. If you've been soaking your clams, swirl them in the water, rinse, drain and leave in the colander. Heat your barbecue coals. It is best to cook the fish in racks, otherwise place a grill over the coals. Slash the whole fish and brush on both sides with the lemon oil, then sprinkle well with coarse salt. Cook the butterflied fish, skin side down, then turn and brush the other side with lemon oil. Cook until nicely charred here and there with cooked white flesh. Add any other fish you want to cook to the grill as your butterflied fish cooks so that everything is ready at the same time: whole sardines will probably need to go on next followed by fish fillets, and then clams for the last few minutes. Sit the clams directly on the rack until they open right up.

Once all your fish is perfectly cooked, serve it immediately, splashed with a little more lemon oil, and lemon halves if you like. Add a few drops of lemon juice to the clams or just eat them as they are, straight from the shells. Grill the bread on both sides and drizzle with a little of the lemon oil. Serve with the fish grill.

**SERVES 4–6**

**LEMON OIL**
30 g (1 oz) butter

2 garlic cloves, chopped

a pinch of sweet paprika

a pinch of ground piri piri

¾ teaspoon tomato paste (concentrated purée)

125 ml (4 fl oz/½ cup) olive oil

juice of 1 lemon

1 teaspoon chopped flat-leaf parsley

a couple of handfuls of big clams in their shells

2 x 400 g (14 oz) long slim fish, such as mackerel, trevally or mullet, cleaned and gutted

2 x 400 g (14 oz) plumper fish, such as bream, bass or snapper, butterflied

a few sardines, cleaned and gutted

1–2 thick fish fillets, such as perch, swordfish, snapper, cod or soaked salt cod

coarse salt

lemon halves, to serve

slices of white country-style bread

# ROAST OCTOPUS IN RED WINE WITH POTATOES

This deep and wonderfully flavoured dish was one of the most stunning things I saw while on holiday in Portugal, and I wanted to make it as soon as I got home. Some bread for the leftover sauce is fundamental. The last half an hour of cooking is vital — the octopus needs to soften in the oven first, then roast until it is a bit crusty. Don't take it out too early when it still looks like a boiled dish.

To clean the octopus, cut between the head and tentacles, just below the eyes. Grasp the body and push the beak up and out through the centre of the tentacles with your finger. Cut the eyes from the head. To clean the head, carefully slit through one side, avoiding the ink sac, and scrape out any gut. Rinse under running water to remove any grit. Cut the head into thick slices and the tentacles into 6 cm (2½ inch) longish pieces on the diagonal.

Preheat your oven to 200°C (400°F/Gas 6). Heat the oil in a non-stick pan. Sauté the onion until sticky, add the garlic and cook until you can smell it. Add the parsley, sauté for a moment then add the tomatoes. Season well, add the piri piri and let it bubble up. Simmer for a couple of minutes, squashing down the tomato lumps, then remove from the heat.

Put the octopus and potatoes in a 28 x 18 cm (11¼ x 7 inch) oven dish that will fit everything in one layer quite compactly. Scrape the tomato mixture over it. Pour in the wine, shuffle everything, and season with salt. Cover with foil and cook for nearly an hour or until the octopus is tender and the potatoes are nicely cooked if you poke a fork into one.

Remove the foil, turn the oven down to 180°C (350°F/Gas 4) and cook for 30 minutes or more until the top is deep roasty-looking here and there, and there is an abundance of almost jammy-looking sauce. Serve with lots of bread for that sauce.

SERVES 4–6

500–600 g (about 1 lb 4 oz) octopus

5 tablespoons olive oil

1 onion, chopped

2–3 garlic cloves, chopped

2–3 heaped tablespoons chopped flat-leaf parsley

400 g (14 oz) tinned chopped tomatoes

a pinch of ground piri piri

600 g (1 lb 5 oz) potatoes, peeled and cut into largish chunks

185 ml (6 fl oz/¾ cup) red wine

# SOLE BUNDLES
# WITH SPINACH

This is nice with mash or chips, or just on its own with some bread. If you can't get sole, use fillets from another white-fleshed fish such as whiting, silver dory or flounder. They need to be long fillets — fine-flaked, narrow and about 5 mm (¼ inch) thick so that they can be rolled easily.

SERVES 4

Heat 3 tablespoons of the oil and a garlic clove in a non-stick deep-sided frying pan that will hold all the sole bundles later on. Add the tomatoes and basil, season lightly with salt and simmer over low heat for about 10 minutes, or until everything has melted together into a sauce.

Heat the remainder of the oil with the other garlic clove in a saucepan and add the spinach. Sauté for a few minutes to wilt the leaves. Remove from the heat, season with salt and stir in the parmesan. Fish out the garlic clove.

Lay the fish fillets on a flat surface, former-skin side down. Put about a teaspoon of the spinach mixture onto the tapered end of each fillet and roll up the fish compactly around the spinach. Secure with toothpicks. Roll the fish bundles in flour to coat lightly. Arrange them in a single layer over the tomato sauce in the pan and sprinkle with a little extra salt.

Put the lid on the pan and simmer for 5 minutes or so, until the undersides of the fish bundles become lightly golden. Very gently turn them over, sprinkle with salt and put the lid back on. Simmer for another 5 minutes, or until the inside of the fish is cooked. If the sauce seems at all dry, add a few drops of hot water and heat through. Serve with lemon wedges.

4 tablespoons olive oil

2 garlic cloves, peeled and squashed a bit

200 g (7 oz) tinned chopped tomatoes

2 basil leaves, torn

150 g (5½ oz) English spinach leaves, chopped

30 g (1 oz) grated parmesan cheese

8 sole fillets without skin

plain (all-purpose) flour, for dusting

lemon wedges, to serve

# PAN-FRIED SOLE WITH LEMON GARLIC BUTTER

This sauce is also very good over a grilled (broiled) chicken breast or steak. You can make as much or as little of it as you need, but I try to have at least two generous tablespoons per serving. Your fishmonger should be able to skin the fish when he guts them (and you can use different fish, if you prefer). It's best to decide beforehand how you are going to serve the sole — you can cook them ready-filleted, or cook them whole and serve with sauce spooned over and let everyone fillet their own on their plate. They come away from the bone easily, but it's still always worth double-checking for tiny missed bones. They do look impressive served whole — so often I serve them like that, then move the fish to a clean empty plate, quickly fillet it and return the fillets to the plate of sauce. You will need to work quickly, so have everything ready before you start.

For the sauce, put the butter and garlic in a small pan and cook over medium heat until sizzling. Add the paprika, season well with salt, and sizzle a bit more so that the flavours mingle. When it starts looking a bit golden brown, add the lemon juice and cook for a minute longer. Keep warm.

Sprinkle the flour over a plate and lightly pat both sides of the fish in it. Heat the butter in a large non-stick frying pan and add the fish. Cook over medium–high heat until their undersides are nicely golden. Sprinkle with salt and then gently flip them over. Salt the cooked side and fry until the new underside is golden. Cover the pan with a lid now and cook for a few minutes to make sure the fish are cooked through. If you think there is not enough butter or it is browning too much, then add another blob of butter to the pan. Remove the fish to plates.

Add about 2 tablespoons of your sauce to the frying pan and heat through to collect the pan flavours. Spoon over the fish and sprinkle with parsley. Serve immediately, with the remaining warm sauce spooned over.

**SERVES 2**

**SAUCE**
40 g (1½ oz) butter

2 garlic cloves, peeled and squashed a bit

¼ teaspoon sweet paprika

juice of 1 lemon

about 4 tablespoons plain (all-purpose) flour

2 whole sole (about 200 g/7 oz each), skinned and gutted

30 g (1 oz) butter

1 tablespoon chopped flat-leaf parsley

# SCAMPI SOUR

You could add two tablespoons of pine nuts and raisins to the onion, or even use leek instead of onion. The scampi (langoustines) must be lovely and fresh and if you had beautiful fresh sardines, these flavours would also complement them.

SERVES 4

Peel the scampi. Remove the tail meat by cutting down the centre of the underside of the tail with small sharp scissors and using your fingers to pull out the meat. Devein, wash, pat dry and leave in the fridge.

Heat the oil in a non-stick frying pan with a lid and cook the onion for a few minutes before adding the peppercorns, bay leaves and some salt. Cover, lower the heat and simmer for 20–25 minutes until well softened but not browned. Check from time to time that not all the liquid has been absorbed. Add the wine, let it bubble up a bit, then add the vinegar and simmer, uncovered now, for another 5–10 minutes until it has reduced a bit and its intensity has cooked out but it is still good and saucy rather than dry.

Put some flour on a plate and coat the scampi well. Pour enough oil into a large non-stick frying pan to cover the bottom abundantly. When the oil is hot add the scampi, turning them only when they are crisp on the bottom. If the flour is falling off the scampi and sticking to the bottom, you may need to reduce the heat a touch. When both sides are golden and quite crisp remove to a plate lined with paper towel to absorb the oil. Sprinkle with fine salt.

Put half the onion in a small bowl, top with the scampi and cover with the remaining onion. Scatter some pepper here and there. Add a splash more oil if you think it needs it.

Cover and either leave at room temperature if you will be eating within the next few hours, or put in the fridge where they will keep for a few days, soaking up the flavours more and more.

18–20 scampi (langoustines, red-claw or large prawns)

125 ml (4 fl oz/½ cup) olive oil

400 g (14 oz) white onions, halved and thinly sliced

a few whole black peppercorns, squashed a bit

2 bay leaves

3 tablespoons white wine

125 ml (4 fl oz/½ cup) white wine vinegar

plain (all-purpose) flour, for coating

light olive oil, for frying

# MUSSELS WITH FETA & PEPPERS

Greek peppers (capsicums) are beautiful. Red and pale green. Small and long. Thin fleshed. A couple of them here, sliced in rings, give a great flavour. If you can't find those then use a similar weight of other small sweet peppers.

This dish can also be served with the mussels shelled, but I love shells on. Make sure your mussels are fresh. Serve with bread.

De-beard the mussels. Scrub them with a wire brush under cold running water, then drain. Give each one a tap and discard those that stay open. Heat the oil in a pot large enough to take the mussels and which has a lid. Sauté the peppers until softened. Add the garlic and dried ground chilli and when it smells good, add the mussels. Put the lid on, turn up the heat and cook for just a minute or so until the mussels open. Give the ones that haven't opened another chance to open, but then discard those that still have not opened. Add the lemon juice, put the lid back on and give the pot a shake.

Scatter the feta over the top, return the lid and shake the pan again. Leave for a minute for the feta to soften but don't let it dissolve, it's nice to be able to see soft chunks of feta here and there. Add the parsley and a few good grinds of black pepper and turn the mussels through gently. Serve hot.

**SERVES 6 OR SO**

about 1.5 kg (3 lb 5 oz) black mussels

5 tablespoons olive oil

1 small red sweet pepper (capsicum) (about 40 g/1½ oz), seeded and sliced into thin rings

1 small green sweet pepper (capsicum)(about 40 g/1½ oz), seeded and sliced into thin rings

2 garlic cloves, chopped

pinch of dried ground chilli

juice of 2 lemons

200 g (7 oz) feta, roughly chopped

4 tablespoons chopped flat-leaf parsley

# FISH PIE

This is Harriet's — my mum's friend in Finland — a wonderful, stylish lady and cook. I tasted this many years ago and have always remembered it. Her original recipe uses pike-perch fillets, but you can use any fish fillets you like, just make sure they have no bones. In this pie the mash is only around the rim, not covering the whole thing, and it is important to use a dish that is no deeper than 6 cm (2½ inches). Maybe make a few smoked salmon crostini for a starter and serve a green salad and bread with your pie and that really is a complete family dinner, I feel.

For the sauce, melt the butter in a smallish saucepan and then stir in the flour. Cook for a minute or so over medium heat and then add the broth, whisking well to make a smooth sauce. Let it bubble up for a few minutes and then stir in the cream. Taste for salt and pepper (your broth will probably be seasoned already).

Preheat the oven to 200°C (400°F/Gas 6) and butter a 32 x 22 x 6 cm (13 x 8½ x 2½ inch) ovenproof dish. Heat 20 g (¾ oz) of the butter and the garlic in a frying pan and, when it is sizzling, add the mushrooms and a little salt. Sauté over high heat, shifting the mushrooms around with a wooden spoon until all their juices have evaporated and they have turned golden. Add the wine and some pepper and cook until the wine has evaporated. Remove from the heat.

Cut the fish into large chunks of about 5–6 cm (2½ inches) and put in the bottom of your dish. Scrape the mushrooms out over the fish, then add the prawns. Scatter with the parsley and a few grinds of pepper. Pour the sauce over the top. Bake for about 20 minutes or until the sauce is bubbling and a bit golden here and there.

Meanwhile, boil the potatoes in salted water until soft. Heat the remaining butter in the milk. Drain the potatoes and mash them or pass them through a potato mill into a bowl. Beat in the rest of the butter and the warm milk and season, if necessary.

Arrange the mash in dollops just around the rim of the dish, then bake the pie for another 10 minutes or so, or until the mash is a little golden in places. Leave it to stand for 5–10 minutes before serving with lemon wedges.

SERVES 5

SAUCE
30 g (1 oz) butter
30 g (1 oz) plain (all-purpose) flour
300 ml (10½ fl oz) vegetable broth, warmed
100 ml (3½ fl oz) pouring (single) cream

60 g (2¼ oz) butter
1 garlic clove, peeled and squashed a bit
200 g (7 oz) button mushrooms, sliced
2 tablespoons white wine
500 g (1 lb 2 oz) skinless halibut, cod or snapper fillets
500 g (1 lb 2 oz) raw prawns (shrimp), peeled and deveined
2 tablespoons chopped flat-leaf parsley
1 kg (2 lb 4 oz) potatoes, peeled and cut into chunks
185 ml (6 fl oz/¾ cup) milk, warmed
lemon wedges, to serve

# 7

~ MEAT ~

# CHICKEN ESCALOPES WITH TOMATOES & CAPERS

This is the kind of dish my mother-in-law has taught me to make — she is such an inspiration. You can add a couple of olives or anything else you think might be appreciated. I like to serve this with some pan-fried chips with rosemary and sage or even just my favourite bread. Buy chicken escalopes from your butcher, or buy one chicken breast and thinly slice it horizontally into four escalopes.

Heat half the oil with the garlic in a large non-stick frying pan. Add the tomatoes with a little salt and fry over high heat until they are just starting to pucker. Lift them out onto a plate.

Add the remaining oil to the pan. Lightly dust the chicken with flour on both sides. Put into the pan, add the sage and fry over medium–high heat until the undersides are golden. Turn over and season with salt. Put the garlic cloves on top of the chicken if they look in danger of burning. Cook until the new underside is golden brown, then turn the chicken again and season with salt. Add the wine, put the tomatoes on top of the chicken escalopes and throw in the capers and parsley. Let it bubble up and evaporate a bit, then put on the lid and leave for a couple of minutes before serving.

**SERVES 2**

about 4 tablespoons olive oil

2 garlic cloves, peeled and squashed a bit

150 g (5½ oz) cherry tomatoes, halved

4 chicken escalopes

plain (all-purpose) flour, for dusting

2 sage sprigs

3 tablespoons white wine or water

1 tablespoon drained capers in vinegar, rinsed

1 tablespoon chopped flat-leaf parsley

# ROAST CHICKEN & POTATOES WITH THYME, LEMON & GARLIC

This is a lovely roast chicken ... with just a dash of cream to bring everything and everyone together. You will need to use a roasting tin that can also be put on the stovetop to heat up the sauce. If you don't have anything suitable, you can transfer all the chicken juices to a small saucepan.

Preheat the oven to 200°C (400°F/Gas 6). Wipe the chicken with paper towel and put, breast side down, in a large roasting tin. Put a little salt, a garlic clove, 3 of the thyme sprigs and 1 of the bay leaves in the cavity of the chicken. Scatter the potatoes and remaining garlic around and pour the lemon juice over the top. Rub the skin of the chicken with some of the butter and dot the rest over the potatoes. Bury the rest of the thyme sprigs under the potatoes, then sprinkle salt over the potatoes and the chicken. Pour 250 ml (9 fl oz/1 cup) of water around the edge of the dish.

Roast for about 1 hour or until the chicken is nicely golden, then turn it over and shuffle the potatoes around. Spoon the pan juices over the top of the chicken and potatoes and scatter some salt over the new top of the chicken. Roast for about 30 minutes, shuffling the potatoes around again halfway through without breaking them up too much, or until the chicken is deep golden and crispy and its juices run clear. Transfer the chicken to a generous serving platter with a bit of a raised edge and arrange the potatoes around the chicken. Keep warm.

Put the roasting tin of cooking juices over medium heat on the stovetop.

Using a wooden spoon, scrape up all the golden bits from the sides and bottom of the tin. If there isn't much liquid, add 3–4 tablespoons of water. Bring to the boil and cook until slightly thickened. Stir the cream through and let it all bubble up, whisking so it all comes together as one. Pour over the chicken on the platter and serve immediately.

**SERVES 4**

1 chicken (about 1.6 kg/3 lb 8 oz)

4 garlic cloves, peeled but left whole

about 10 thyme sprigs

3 bay leaves (fresh, if possible)

1 kg (2 lb 4 oz) potatoes, peeled and cut into chunks

juice of 2 lemons

60 g (2¼ oz) butter, softened

3 tablespoons thin (pouring) cream

# FRIED CHICKEN

This is another great chicken recipe that makes two dishes in one go: fried chicken and a chicken soup. Use the broth to cook some pasta or rice and make a soupy meal. You can also add an extra egg to the leftover marinade and make a quick omelette for after your soup.

SERVES 4

Rinse the chicken and put in a large saucepan with the sage, carrot, celery and one garlic clove. Cover with 1 litre (35 fl oz/4 cups) of cold water and season with salt. Bring to the boil, uncovered, then lower the heat slightly to medium. Simmer for another 15 minutes, then remove from the heat. The chicken will be just boiled, not overcooked.

Remove the chicken with a slotted spoon to a plate and pat dry with paper towel. (At this stage you're left with the basis of a very good chicken broth in the saucepan. Add another cupful of water and simmer the soup for another 45 minutes. Store in the fridge or freezer until needed.)

Whip the eggs in a shallow bowl. Finely chop the remaining garlic and add to the egg with the paprika and a little salt. Put the chicken pieces in the egg, turning to coat them well, then leave to marinate for 10–15 minutes.

Put the flour on a flat plate. Heat enough oil for shallow-frying in a frying pan or wide saucepan. Lift the chicken out of the marinade, shaking off any excess egg, then pat in the flour, pressing down gently with your palm so that the flour sticks. Fry the chicken in the hot oil until it is deeply golden and crispy on both sides. Serve with lemon wedges, if you like.

1 x 1.25 kg (2 lb 12 oz) chicken with skin, cut into 8 pieces

3 sage leaves

1 carrot, cut into 2 or 3 chunks

1 celery stalk, cut into 3 or 4 chunks

2 garlic cloves

2 eggs

½ teaspoon sweet paprika

90 g (3¼ oz) plain (all-purpose) flour

light olive oil or vegetable oil, for shallow-frying

# SAUTÉED CHICKEN WITH BAY LEAVES & JUNIPER BERRIES

The fresh bay leaves give a wonderful flavour and smell. With a simple pan of boiled potatoes with parsley and green vegetables sautéed in olive oil and garlic, this is the kind of thing I would present to my family on a cool autumn night.

SERVES 4

Put the oil, bay leaves and juniper berries in a large non-stick frying pan or flameproof casserole. Put the chicken on the bay leaves, turn the heat to medium and put the lid on the casserole. Cook until the underside of the chicken is lightly golden and the top is white. Turn over and salt and pepper the done side. Add 1 or 2 tablespoons of hot water if the chicken looks like sticking, then cover and cook until the juices have all evaporated. Turn again and salt and pepper lightly.

Squash the juniper berries with a fork to release the flavour, but still keep them fairly intact. Pour in the wine and cook uncovered until the wine has evaporated and the chicken is deep golden on all sides. When there is very little liquid in the pan, and even the bay leaves seem covered by some crusty sauce, turn off the heat, cover and leave to stand for 10 minutes or so before serving.

3 tablespoons olive oil

8 fresh bay leaves

25 juniper berries

1 chicken, cut into 10 pieces, skin removed

125 ml (4 fl oz/½ cup) white wine

# GRILLED CHICKEN PIRI PIRI

This is fantastic. I made it in the Algarve with the wonderful cook Teresa, who I was lucky to find. Thank you, Teresa! It's important to use small chickens or they will have burnt on the outside before they've cooked through. If yours are on the larger side, make sure you slash the flesh well so they cook through.

If necessary, you can make one of the chickens child-friendly by not brushing with the piri piri but, instead, basting it with the lemon garlic marinade while it cooks. The piri piri will strengthen as it sits, so make it fiery enough for your own tastes.

Rinse the chickens and pat dry. Cut each chicken in half so you have four pieces (you can butterfly them, but smaller pieces are easier to cook). Cut off the wing tips and cut a little way into the bone joints so they crack open and flatten to help the chicken cook evenly. Make a couple of slashes where the meat is thickest to be sure that it cooks all the way through.

To make the marinade, cut the lemon in half and squeeze the juice into a bowl that will fit the chickens. Throw in the lemon halves, garlic, oregano, paprika and then the chickens, scattering generously with coarse salt. Turn it all together well and massage into the chickens.

Leave covered (but not in the fridge) for at least half an hour until the chicken has taken in the salt (if you're leaving it longer you'll need to put it in the fridge). Heat the barbecue with a grill 15 cm (6 inches) from the hot coals.

To make the basting sauce, pulse the chillies and garlic to a rough paste in a food processor (or use a mortar and pestle). Heat the butter and oil with the paste in a small pan until it is sizzling and you start to smell the garlic. Add the salt, lemon juice, bay leaf, port and whisky and let it bubble up for 5 minutes, then remove from the heat. Taste and add more ground piri piri, if you like.

Shake the chickens out of the marinade and place, skin side up, on the grill. (If the fat drips and causes flames, remove the rack and extinguish the fire with ash or water, otherwise the skin will burn and taste terrible.)

Turn the chickens when the first side is cooked. After 25 minutes or so, when they're almost ready, start basting with the piri piri. Baste a couple of times on each side. Cut each chicken half into four (it's nicer to serve this way and you can check that the bits closer to the bone are cooked) and drizzle with the rest of the piri piri sauce. Serve with tomato rice or chips and salad.

**SERVES 4**

2 x 800 g (1 lb 12 oz) chickens

**MARINADE**
1 lemon
3–4 garlic cloves, finely chopped
1 teaspoon dried oregano
1 teaspoon sweet paprika
coarse salt

**PIRI PIRI BASTING SAUCE**
6–8 small dried piri piri chillies (or 3–4 fresh)
3 garlic cloves, roughly chopped
70 g (2½ oz) butter
2 tablespoons olive oil
1 teaspoon fine salt
juice of 1 lemon
1 bay leaf
2 tablespoons ruby port
2 tablespoons whisky
extra ground piri piri (optional)

# LUDI'S CHICKEN

This is my sister Tanja's recipe. Ludi is a nickname: she calls me Ludi, and I call her Ludi (our children often look puzzled). This dish just seems to work for all ages and however many people happen to end up eating. You can even serve it at room temperature and the potatoes still end up tasting good — which is not a common thing for roast potatoes, really.

Preheat the oven to 180°C (350°F/Gas 4). Halve the potatoes lengthways and then cut them into three or four pieces so that they look like giant chips.

Mix together the mustard, lemon juice, oregano and olive oil to make a marinade. Put the chicken, potatoes, onion wedges, bay leaves and 4 of the garlic cloves in a large oven dish. Season the potatoes and chicken (outside and in the cavity) with salt and pepper. Put two of the squeezed lemon halves and the remaining garlic in the chicken cavity. Splash the marinade over the chicken and potatoes, shuffling them around with your hands so they are well coated. Gently pour a cupful of water into the dish (trying not to wash away the marinade). Roast for about 1 hour.

After an hour the top of the chicken should be getting brown. Pour the wine over the top, turn the potatoes and onions, and roast for another hour, turning the chicken when it is well browned on top. Check that the potatoes are still in a little liquid — if they look dry, add a little more hot water.

The chicken should be golden brown, juicy and cooked through. If it seems done but you think the potatoes might need longer, remove the chicken to a warmed serving platter. The potatoes, however, should not be crispy but golden and juicy and there should be a little sauce in the dish to serve with the chicken. If it is dry, add some hot water to the dish and scrape the bits from the bottom and sides to make more sauce. Serve hot or even at room temperature.

SERVES 4

4–5 large potatoes, peeled

2 heaped tablespoons grainy mustard

juice of 2 lemons (but save the squeezed lemon halves)

1 tablespoon dried oregano or thyme, crumbled

4 tablespoons olive oil

1 medium-sized chicken (about 1.3 kg/3 lb)

2 red onions, peeled and cut into wedges

2 bay leaves

6 garlic cloves, with their skin left on

125 ml (4 fl oz/½ cup) white wine

# SAUSAGES & POLENTA

This is a simple and rich dish; the kind of thing you won't see on restaurant menus but that Venetians would make at home to eat in front of a wintry fire. Use good pork sausages, and I like to use a mixture of lardo and pancetta here. Lardo is rather a precious thing — 'lardo di colonnato' is a traditional Tuscan delicacy of cured pork fat and it is prized all over Italy. When sliced very thinly, the majority of the slice is pork fat with just a tiny piece of prosciutto-type meat. Pancetta is very well cured pork, much drier and with much more meat than lardo. Together they are a great combination. You'll need about three thin slices of lardo and four of pancetta. I use white wine here but red is also good. Serve this rich dish with polenta and perhaps a nice plate of radicchio or cabbage.

Sauté the pancetta and lardo in a dry frying pan over heat until some of the oil seeps out, then add the sausages. Cook the sausages until getting slightly golden in places. Remove the pancetta and lardo to a side plate so it won't become too crisp and add the onion to the pan. Cook until your onion is golden and soft (your sausages might not yet look lovely and brown but they will have more time in the pan later).

Return the pancetta and lardo to the pan and fry for a few minutes until everything is nicely melded together. Add the wine and simmer for 30 minutes, turning the sausages over once when they are golden on the bottom, the wine has evaporated and things once again look as if they are frying in the oil. If you won't be serving immediately, cover with a lid. Serve a sausage and some of the sauce and rich oil over a serving of polenta. Scatter with parmesan.

**SERVES 6**

about 60 g (2¼ oz) thinly sliced pancetta, chopped

about 60 g (2¼ oz) thinly sliced lardo, chopped

6 good pork sausages (about 650 g/ 1 lb 7 oz), pricked all over

1 small onion, sliced

250 ml (9 fl oz/1 cup) white wine

polenta and grated parmesan cheese, to serve

TESSA KIROS ~ THE RECIPE COLLECTION

# SAUSAGE & POTATO FRITTATA

I like this for a Sunday breakfast or supper with wholemeal (wholewheat) bread. If you think your children won't enjoy the vegetables here, you could make it with just the sausage, potatoes and parsley — or anything else you know will be appreciated.

SERVES 6–8

Boil the potatoes in their skins in lightly salted water until they are tender but not breaking up. Drain, cool and then cut into chunks, keeping the skins on. Put to one side for now.

Heat 2 tablespoons of the oil in a 26 cm (10½ inch) non-stick ovenproof frying pan over medium heat and fry the sausage meat until it is quite deeply golden, breaking up clusters with a wooden spoon. Lift out into a bowl with a slotted spoon. Add the onion to the pan and sauté until golden, then add the carrot. Sauté for 5 minutes or so, until both become soft and a bit gooey. Add another tablespoon of oil and the mushrooms and sauté until the mushrooms have given up their water and turned golden. Season lightly if needed. Spoon the contents of the pan into the bowl with the sausage.

Preheat the grill (broiler) to medium–high. Add the last of the oil to the pan and sauté the potatoes until they have a golden crust in some places. Stir in the parsley and the contents of the sausage bowl and cook for a minute or two. Reduce the heat to medium–low and pour in the eggs, shifting everything around with a wooden spoon so that the eggs leak under here and there. Once the bottom looks softly set, put the pan under the grill so that the frittata sets just enough to be cut into slices. Don't overdo it though, as this is nice when it is still a little soft. Serve warm with your favourite bread.

2 small potatoes, scrubbed

5 tablespoons olive oil

375 g (13 oz) Italian sausage, skinned and crumbled

1 red onion, chopped

1 carrot, peeled and chopped

80 g (2¾ oz) button mushrooms, finely sliced

4 tablespoons chopped flat-leaf parsley

6 eggs, lightly beaten

# MINCE & RICE DUMPLINGS WITH DILL, EGG & LEMON SAUCE

These are wonderfully soft meat and rice dumplings that most Greek children eat on a regular basis. If you think that the dill might not be appreciated, then you can leave it out — but it does give a special and definite flavour.

For the dumplings, put the minced meat, oregano, dill, parsley, egg, rice and onion in a mixing bowl with the milk and season well with salt. Knead with your hands so it is all very well mixed. Shape the dumplings by breaking off chunks about the size of a large walnut and quickly patting them into balls or ovals.

Heat the oil and garlic in a non-stick frying pan and fry the dumplings in batches over medium–high heat, turning them carefully when they are lightly golden on the underside, and lifting the dumplings into a large flameproof casserole when they are golden all over.

When all the dumplings are in the casserole, gently pour in 1.25 litres (44 fl oz/5 cups) of hot water. Add a little extra salt and bring to a gentle boil. Lower the heat to a bare simmer, cover with a lid and cook for an hour. There should be a fair amount of liquid still at the end. Remove from the heat.

For the sauce, whip the egg in a bowl and then whisk in the lemon juice and a pinch of salt. Add a ladleful of the hot liquid from the casserole (which you will have to tip to the side to get to). Quickly whisk the hot liquid into the egg mixture to acclimatise the eggs, then add another couple of ladlefuls along with the dill, mixing well.

With the casserole off the heat, pour all the egg and lemon sauce back in, quickly hula-hooping the casserole around to shift everything so that the eggs don't scramble. Cover and let it sit for a few minutes — there should be enough heat left in the casserole to just cook the eggs through. Taste that there is enough salt before serving, perhaps adding a grinding of black pepper. Best served warm, but also good at room temperature.

SERVES 5–6

**DUMPLINGS**

1 kg (2 lb 4 oz) minced (ground) pork and veal

½ teaspoon oregano

3 tablespoons chopped dill

3 tablespoons chopped flat-leaf parsley

1 egg

160 g (5½ oz) rice

1 large red onion, grated

150 ml (5 fl oz) milk

3–4 tablespoons olive oil

2 garlic cloves, peeled but left whole

**SAUCE**

1 egg

juice of 2 lemons

2 tablespoons chopped dill

# BAKED PORK RIBS
# WITH ORANGE

I ate this one night in Ponte Delgada on the island of San Miguel.
I asked the chef and this is more or less the recipe he gave me. I was
very happy to come home and make it. This makes a big dish of ribs
but you just bang it in the oven and it's a lovely, easy way to feed a
crowd. If you want to make less, just reduce the amount of ribs, or
you could make them all anyway and have leftovers for the next day.

**SERVES 6**

Preheat your oven to 180°C (350°F/Gas 4). Cut the pork ribs into single ribs
and trim off excess fat (you should get about 16 ribs). Heat 3 tablespoons
of the oil in a large non-stick frying pan and cook the ribs until well browned
on the undersides. Turn and cook until deep golden all over (do this in
batches if necessary). Add the bay leaves at the end, season and add the wine
and orange juice. Let it bubble away for a few minutes, then turn off the heat.
Meanwhile, heat the remaining oil in a small frying pan and sauté the onion
until beautifully golden. Add the garlic and, when you start to smell it, add
the tomatoes. Bubble up for a moment, stir in the piri piri, if you like, and
turn off the heat.

Find a roasting tin that will fit everything snugly in one layer. Put an orange
quarter in each corner and dot the rest here and there. Arrange the ribs in one
layer and scrape the tomato mixture over them, turning through the ribs and
even over the orange quarters. Roast for about 30 minutes until tender and
golden and dotted with bits of sauce. Serve hot.

1 kg (2 lb 4 oz) short pork ribs

125 ml (4 fl oz/½ cup) olive oil

2 bay leaves

125 ml (4 fl oz/½ cup) white wine

juice of 1 orange, plus 2 oranges,
   quartered

1 large white onion, chopped

3 garlic cloves, chopped

3 tablespoons tinned chopped
   tomatoes

a pinch of ground piri piri (optional)

# PORK SKEWERS

These can either be wrapped in pita with tzatziki (see page 241), tomatoes, lemon and parsley, as in the kebabs (see page 209), or served as is on the stick with some grilled bread. Here then, extra oregano and salt should be scattered on and lemon wedges served on the side. Use a part of the pork towards the shoulder where it's more tender. Pork fillets also work very well, just make sure you don't dry out the meat in the grilling as they have little fat.

Soak the skewers in cold water for about 30 minutes so they won't burn when they go over the coals. Trim any drastic fat off the pork but leave some on for flavour and moistness. Cut the meat into rough 2 cm (¾ inch) cubes. Thread 6 pork cubes onto each skewer, leaving space at the top to spike the bread.

Put the skewers onto a plate, sprinkle with the oregano that you crush between your fingers, a little salt and some pepper. Drizzle the oil over and turn to coat evenly.

Preheat the barbecue to high and put the rack about 10 cm (4 inches) from the coals. Grill the skewers until nice and grilled–looking here and there and still moist, not dry inside. Grill the bread lightly on both sides and spike it on the end of the skewers. Serve on a plate, or on squares of baking paper, scattering over some extra salt and crushing over some extra oregano. Serve hot, with lemon juice squeezed over.

**MAKES ABOUT 12 SKEWERS**

wooden skewers

1.2 kg (2 lb 10 oz) lean pork with some fat

2 teaspoons dried oregano, plus extra to serve

3 tablespoons olive oil

about 12 slices of country-style bread (about 2 cm/¾ inch thick), halved if large

about 2 lemons, quartered

# LAMB & BEEF KEBABS

There are foods that are taken from neighbouring countries and immigration that then become a fixed item, such as kebabs, which have Turkish origins. The mince here should have a little fat and the kebabs must be cooked over very hot coals so that they are nicely charred but still moist inside. If you don't have the skewers, you can just pat the meat into sausage shapes and grill anyway. Eating two of these in pita is not unreasonable if you are not having anything else. The thing about eating these is that the warm juice runs the length of the meat into the pita, like a small stream in a current, and pools in the bottom, dripping inevitably through the soaked paper onto your hand. So you will need some aeroplane-like wet towels — or simply apologise to the next batch of people you are introduced to or run into and have to kiss on both cheeks.

Put the minces, grated onion, parsley and oregano in a bowl and add the salt. Knead together thoroughly. Divide into eight balls of about 80 g (2¾ oz) each. Firmly press each ball compactly around a skewer in a long sausage shape of about 15 cm (6 inches) long. Thread 4 tomato quarters on each of the remaining skewers, making sure that you pierce through the skin so that they hold well.

Preheat the grill to high and brush it lightly with olive oil. Grill the meat kebabs until deep golden and slightly crusty in parts on the outside and still moist on the inside, but not dried out. Brush the tomatoes with a little olive oil, scatter lightly with salt and pepper and grill them at the same time. Brush the pita very lightly with olive oil on both sides (or leave plain if you prefer) and put on the grill to warm up.

To serve, remove the skewers from the kebabs. Halve the tomato quarters. Put a square of baking paper on each plate and then 1 pita on top of each of these. Add a meat kebab, a couple of pieces of tomato, some onion slices, a good amount of parsley, a nice dab of tzatziki, a squeeze of lemon juice and a shaking of paprika. Add salt if you like. Roll up the pita quite tightly then roll the paper around. Tuck the bottom in and leave the top third of the pita out. Eat. Move on to your second one. Then follow with a nice ice cream.

SERVES 4

**KEBABS**
250 g (9 oz) finely minced (ground) lamb

250 g (9 oz) finely minced (ground) beef

1 small red onion, grated

2 tablespoons coarsely chopped flat-leaf parsley

½ teaspoon dried oregano, crumbled

¾–1 teaspoon salt

12 thick metal skewers

3 tomatoes (about 120 g/4¼ oz each), quartered

olive oil, for brushing

8 pita bread

8 squares baking paper, roughly 25 cm (10 inches) 1 small red onion (about 80 g/2¾ oz), sliced

a couple of handfuls coarsely chopped flat-leaf parsley

tzatziki (see page 241), to serve

lemon quarters, to serve

sweet paprika in a shaker, to serve

# LAMB & GREEN BEAN CASSEROLE

I like to make this in advance and then leave it in the oven to cool down completely. This seems to make the meat even softer, and then I just warm it up a bit on the stovetop to serve. This is a great one-pot meal that needs just the time to prepare and chop up the ingredients, and not much more attention from then on. You can use chunks of lamb or beef here, and throw in a couple of potatoes, cut up into chunks, with the beans, if you like. The green beans alone are also delicious cooked like this; still served with crumblings of feta that melt a little into the tomato sauce.

SERVES 3

Preheat the oven to 180°C (350°F/Gas 4). Heat the oil in a heavy-based flameproof casserole over high heat. When it is very hot, add the meat and brown on all sides. Add the onion and cook, stirring, for a few minutes to soften it. When the onion starts to brown, add the butter and garlic. When you can smell the garlic, add the tomatoes. Season with salt and add the cassia or cinnamon. Add 500 ml (17 fl oz/2 cups) of water and bring to the boil. Put on the lid and put the casserole in the oven.

Cook for 45 minutes or so until the meat is soft, and then add the beans, a little more salt and another 250 ml (9 fl oz/1 cup) of water if it needs it. Mix through well, cover and put the casserole back into the oven for another hour. Remove the lid and cook for another 15 minutes until it turns a little golden on the top. Turn off the oven, put the lid back on and leave the casserole in there for about an hour so that the meat is soft and melting. You can warm it up on the stovetop to serve.

Sprinkle the feta over the hot servings, so that it melts slightly, and serve with chunks of bread.

**2 tablespoons olive oil**

**500 g (1 lb 2 oz) deboned trimmed leg or shoulder of lamb, cut into 4 cm (1½ inch) chunks**

**1 red onion, finely chopped**

**20 g (¾ oz) butter**

**2 garlic cloves, chopped**

**300 g (10½ oz) tinned chopped tomatoes**

**a small piece of cassia bark (or cinnamon)**

**400 g (14 oz) green beans, topped (leave the tails on)**

**200 g (7 oz) feta cheese, cut into small chunks**

# LEG OF LAMB WITH OREGANO & LEMON

This is possibly one of my favourite meals. It is soft, wonderful and meltingly lemony and we would sometimes eat the leftovers for breakfast before school. I'm not sure if this is totally the Greek way of making it — maybe the butter and cooking time are my mother's addition — but this is how it is. My mother says you could cook it overnight: I never have, but I believe her.

**SERVES 6**

1.5 kg (3 lb 5 oz) leg of lamb (on the bone)
juice of 2 lemons
1 tablespoon dried oregano
50 g (1¾ oz) butter
3 tablespoons olive oil
4 large potatoes

Preheat the oven to 220°C (425°F/Gas 7). Rinse and trim the lamb of excess fat and put it in a large baking dish. Rub the lamb all over with the lemon juice, season well with salt and pepper and sprinkle with the oregano, crushing it between your fingers to cover the meat. Dot the butter over the top. Pour 250 ml (9 fl oz/1 cup) of water around the lamb and drizzle the olive oil around it as well. Bake for about 15–30 minutes on each side, until it is browned all over.

Meanwhile, peel the potatoes and cut them into bite-sized pieces. Scatter them in the baking dish around the browned lamb, add some salt and turn them over with a wooden spoon to coat them in the juices. Add a little more water if it has evaporated. Cover the baking dish with foil, lower the heat to 180°C (350°F/Gas 4) and bake for 2½ hours or so, turning the lamb over at least once during this time and shuffling the potatoes. If the lamb isn't browned enough, remove the foil for the final 30 minutes of cooking. Serve warm on a huge platter with a salad or some simply cooked greens. This is also nice with some tzatziki (see page 241) on the side.

# CYPRIOT BAKED LAMB & POTATOES WITH CUMIN & TOMATOES

This is so simple. It's a very typical Cypriot all-in-one meal called *tava* — you just need the time to prepare the lamb and vegetables, then you can fling it in the oven, go out for a (Greek) coffee and come home to a ready meal. You could use lamb chops and leave them whole instead of cutting them into chunks, which makes it even simpler. And it doesn't need much by way of accompaniments — perhaps a salad or some simply sautéed green vegetables.

Preheat your oven to 180°C (350°F/Gas 4). Put the onion, potatoes and lamb in a 5 litre (175 fl oz/20 cup) casserole dish or a deep baking dish. Season with salt and pepper. Add the parsley, cumin seeds and olive oil and mix through very well with your hands. Put the tomato slices on top in a single layer and season lightly with salt. Dot the butter over the top and pour about 125 ml (4 fl oz/½ cup) of water around the sides of the dish. Cover with foil and bake for 2 hours, tilting the dish from side to side a couple of times and spooning some of the pan juices over the top. The lamb should be very tender and the potatoes soft.

Remove the foil, increase the oven temperature to 200°C (400°F/Gas 6) and cook for another 45 minutes or so, turning the lamb halfway through, or until the meat and potatoes are a little browned and the liquid has reduced. Serve hot or at room temperature.

SERVES 6

2 red onions, roughly chopped

1.2 kg (2 lb 10 oz) potatoes, cut into large chunks

1 kg (2 lb 4 oz) lamb, cut into chunks

4 tablespoons chopped flat-leaf parsley

3 heaped teaspoons cumin seeds

125 ml (4 fl oz/½ cup) olive oil

4–5 ripe tomatoes, cut into thick slices

50 g (1¾ oz) butter

# ROASTED LAMB & RICE-SHAPED PASTA

*Youvetsi* is a Greek dish traditionally served on a Sunday. People would put all their ingredients into a large ceramic dish that this recipe is cooked in (the *youvetsi*) and take it to the baker's with a packet of rice-shaped pasta. You could give any specific instructions to the baker, and he would add the pasta in at the end. Discussions would always be that the baker had done well that time, or perhaps it had got a bit too overcooked — but always it was good. And it would always smell like a whole tavern, having caught all the other interesting smells like roasting chickens in the air. This was a good way for the housewife to rest on a Sunday, and one of the family members, such as her husband or son, would go and collect the *youvetsi*. If you don't have a ceramic dish like this, you can use a good wide, round or rectangular dish and if you can't get the small rice-shaped pasta, you can use another type. This dish is often also made with beef, chicken or octopus. Sometimes the pasta is cooked with no meat, just tomato and served with coarsely grated firm *mizithra*.

**SERVES 6**

Preheat the oven to 180°C (350°F/Gas 4). Trim any excess fat off the lamb. Squeeze the lemon juice over and massage it in. Put 4 tablespoons of the olive oil in a large (about 36 cm/14¼ inch diameter) baking dish (or a *youvetsi*, of course, if you have one). Add the lamb, then drizzle the rest of the oil over it. Rub the paprika and garlic onto the lamb and season well with salt and pepper. Add the spring onion, tomatoes, oregano and cinnamon to the dish and sprinkle with some salt too. Put in the oven and roast for 30 minutes. Add 250 ml (9 fl oz/1 cup) of hot water and cook for an hour, turning the lamb halfway through.

In the meantime, boil the pasta in lightly salted water until just done. Drain. When the lamb is done, add the pasta around it in the dish with 375 ml (13 fl oz/1½ cups) of hot water and gently mix into the tomato, trying not to get the pasta on the lamb. Return to the oven for 10–15 minutes, or until the pasta has absorbed quite a bit of the liquid but is still nice and saucy. Remove from the oven and rest in a warm spot for 5 minutes. Grind a little pepper over and take the whole dish to the table for serving, with the cheese on the side for whoever wants some.

1.3–1.5 kg (3–3 lb 5 oz) leg of lamb

½ lemon

125 ml (4 fl oz/½ cup) olive oil

1 teaspoon sweet paprika

2 garlic cloves, finely chopped

150 g (5½ oz) round spring onions (scallions) (about 4), quartered and roughly chopped

400 g (14 oz) tinned chopped tomatoes

¼ teaspoon dried oregano

1 cinnamon stick

250 g (9 oz) *kritharaki* (rice-shaped dried pasta)

grated *kefalotiri*, firm *mizithra* or parmesan cheese, to serve

# COZIDO

Traditionally, this one-pot Portuguese feast uses various exotic meats like pigs' ears and blood sausage. I have chosen some more conservative cuts but you may be as traditional as you wish. On the island of San Miguel in the Azores this is called *cozido à moda das Furnas* — in the town of Furnas it is cooked in a pot in the earth by the heat of the volcanic lava. It's a spectacular sight. I have used an oven here! You'll need a large cast-iron pot for this (mine is about 30 cm/12 inches across and 10 cm/4 inches high) but if your pot is bigger, then even better! Alter the quantities depending on how many will be eating.

SERVES 4–6

Preheat the oven to 200°C (400°F/Gas 6) and cut the pork belly in half. Put the pork belly, pork shoulder, chicken and beef in a cast-iron pot with 125 ml (4 fl oz/½ cup) of water. Put the lid on and put in the oven for 1 hour. Check that nothing is sticking. Reduce the oven to 180°C (350°F/Gas 4) and cook for another 30 minutes.

Wash the beetroot or turnips and cut off the leaves, leaving on a bit of beetroot stem so they don't bleed. Add to the pot with the cabbage slices, carrot, potatoes and sweet potatoes, arranging them beautifully and packing them in tight. Prick the *chouriço* here and there and put it on top to flavour the dish. Season lightly (the beauty is in the mingling of the different meats and vegetables, so don't over-season) and tuck in the cabbage chunks.

Put the lid back on and return to the oven for 1 hour. Check that nothing is sticking by swaying the pot from side to side. Reduce the oven to 150°C (300°F/Gas 2) and cook for another hour. Remove from the oven but leave the lid on. It will be perfect to eat in an hour or so. Serve with white rice or salad and bread.

(Alternatively, if you are near Furnas on the island of San Miguel, just take your pot full of meat and vegetables to be cooked directly in the earth. If you put it in at around 4 am on Sunday, it will be ready around noon … )

450 g (1 lb) slice of raw unsmoked pork belly (pancetta)

450 g (1 lb) slab of pork shoulder, about 5 cm (2 inches) thick

450 g (1 lb) chicken leg and thigh (maryland) with skin

600 g (1 lb 5 oz) boneless piece of beef shin

300 g (10½ oz) baby beetroot (beets) or turnips, or both

¼ of a small cabbage, cut into 2 slices

2 large carrots, peeled and halved

500 g (1 lb 2 oz) potatoes, peeled but left whole

300 g (10½ oz) small sweet potatoes, unpeeled and cut into chunks if large

1 whole *chouriço* sausage (about 180 g/6½ oz)

4 cabbage chunks (any sort: couve, cavolo nero, kale or savoy)

# PAN-FRIED LIVER SCHNITZELS WITH ONIONS

Fried liver was always a regular in traditional old Lisbon taverns and is still today very much appreciated. Liver is an often-overlooked cut, but it makes an economical, quick and delicious meal, especially when cooked quickly and served with piles of sweet sautéed onions.

SERVES 2

300 g (10½ oz) calf liver (or lamb or pork liver, if you prefer)

1 lemon, halved, plus extra to serve

3 garlic cloves, 1 finely chopped, 2 peeled but left whole

about 125 ml (4 fl oz/½ cup) olive oil

1 large onion, thinly sliced

3 bay leaves

about 55 g (2 oz/½ cup) dry breadcrumbs

Wash the liver in cold water, pat dry and cut away any sinew. Slice into 2–3 mm (⅛ inch) thick pieces (I cut up the longer pieces and ended up with five or six schnitzels). Put the liver in a non-metallic bowl, cover with the juice of a lemon half, the chopped garlic and some pepper. Mix well and leave for 30 minutes–2 hours. (Pork liver can be left for longer.)

Heat 5 tablespoons of the oil in a large non-stick frying pan and sauté the onion with a little salt and pepper until sticky and deep golden, adding a bay leaf towards the end. Tip the pan, holding the onion at the top with your wooden spoon so that the oil runs to one side. Scrape the onion onto a plate, leaving the oil in the pan.

Put the breadcrumbs on a plate. Remove the liver from the marinade and pat in the crumbs on both sides. Add another couple of tablespoons of oil to the pan to cover the bottom. Heat up, then add the liver, whole garlic cloves and remaining bay leaves and sprinkle with a little salt.

When the underside of the liver is golden and crusty, turn over with tongs, sprinkling a little salt on the done side. Fry until the underside is golden and crisp and the liver is cooked through but soft as butter inside. If the garlic is burning, sit it on top of the liver.

Squeeze the juice from the other lemon half all around and scrape the onion over the liver. Put the lid on and let it all bubble for a minute. Turn off the heat and leave for a couple of minutes before serving with lots of black pepper and extra lemon halves for those who love lemon.

# PAN-FRIED VEAL CHOPS WITH LEMON, SAGE & MASCARPONE

One of my favourite chefs in the world, Angela Dwyer, taught me this recipe. I love lemon and I love veal, sage and mascarpone, so it is unlikely that I wouldn't love the finished dish. You have to work quickly here so that the butter in the pan doesn't burn and the chops get nicely browned — so have everything ready before you start.

**SERVES 2**

1 tablespoon olive oil

20 g (¾ oz) butter, plus an extra knob

2 veal chops (about 1.5 cm/⅝ inch thick)

6 sage leaves, rinsed and dried

1 garlic clove, crushed

juice of 1 small lemon

60 g (2¼ oz) mascarpone cheese

Heat the oil and butter in a large frying pan. When it is sizzling, add the chops and cook over high heat, turning over when the underneath is golden. Now add the sage leaves and garlic and season the meat with salt and pepper. Add the knob of butter to the pan to prevent burning. Take out the sage leaves when they are crisp and move the garlic around (or take it out if it starts to look too dark). You might like to turn the meat onto its fat side with a pair of tongs so that the fat browns.

Add the lemon juice to the pan and swirl it around, then add the mascarpone. If the veal is cooked, transfer it to a serving plate while you finish the sauce. If you think the veal needs longer, then leave it in the pan. It should be golden brown on the outside and rosy pink, soft, but cooked through on the inside. Add about 3 tablespoons of water to the pan and scrape up all the bits that are stuck to the bottom. Cook for another couple of minutes, then pour the sauce over the veal and scatter with the crispy sage. Serve immediately with some bread for the sauce.

# VEAL INVOLTINI

The veal for this should always be best quality. I usually ask the butcher for four long slices that each weigh about 90 g (3 oz), then cut them in two and bash them out even thinner.

SERVES 4

For the tomato sauce, heat the oil in a pan with the garlic. When you can smell the garlic, add the tomatoes and salt. Mash up a little with a wooden spoon and simmer for about 15 minutes, or until the tomatoes and oil have melted into each other. Add the basil leaves and simmer for another couple of minutes.

Meanwhile, put the veal slices flat on a board. Lay a piece of ham on top of each one, then a slice of mozzarella over the ham. Scatter a teaspoon of parmesan over each one and roll up securely. Stitch them closed with toothpicks, so that the toothpicks lie flat and don't stick up. Don't worry if they all look different. Put the flour on a plate and lightly roll the involtini in it to coat them on all sides. Shake off the excess flour.

Heat the oil in a large frying pan and fry the involtini for just a few minutes, turning them often so that they are golden brown all over. Scatter them with a little salt when they are done, remembering that the tomato sauce is well salted. Leave them in the pan and add the tomato sauce, making sure they are coated. Cover with a lid and simmer for a minute or so. The mozzarella will have softened and started to melt. Remove from the heat but leave the lid on for a minute longer to cook the meat all the way through. Serve immediately, whole or sliced up, with extra toothpicks to use as forks.

**TOMATO SAUCE**

2 tablespoons olive oil

1 garlic clove, peeled and squashed a bit

400 g (14 oz) tinned chopped tomatoes

1 teaspoon salt

3 basil leaves, torn

8 thin veal escalopes (about 2 mm/1⁄16 inch thick)

8 thin slices ham, roughly the same size as the veal

125 g (4½ oz) fresh mozzarella cheese, cut into 8 thin slices

40 g (1½ oz) parmesan cheese, grated

4 tablespoons plain (all-purpose) flour

3 tablespoons olive oil

# LONG-SIMMERED VEAL WITH CREAM & DILL

This might be a real Finnish/Greek combination, but it's what my mother made often. It is quite delicious and just a glance through the ingredients probably makes it sound richer than it is. It is an all-in-one dish that can be taken straight to the table from the stove. You can easily add an extra carrot and potatoes to feed more people: there should be an abundance of sauce.

SERVES 4

Melt the butter with the oil in a large heavy-based flameproof casserole over medium heat. Brown the veal on all sides, salting the browned part. Add the garlic and sauté for another minute. Add the allspice, bay leaf and 1 litre (35 fl oz/4 cups) of water. Lower the heat, cover the casserole and simmer for about 1¼ hours, turning the meat a couple of times. Add the drained potatoes and the carrots. Continue simmering, covered, for another 40 minutes or so, or until the vegetables are nice and soft but not falling apart. Remove from the heat.

Throw away the allspice berries and bay leaf. Remove the meat, slice it fairly thickly and set aside to keep warm on a platter. Remove the vegetables to a warm dish.

Put the flour in a large saucepan and add a ladleful of the hot cooking liquid, stirring with a wooden spoon or whisk until smooth. Add another ladleful and stir in the lemon juice. Put the pan over low heat and add the rest or most of the liquid from the casserole. Cook until it bubbles up, then boil for 7–8 minutes until thickened. Add the cream and dill, heat through and then return all this sauce to the casserole along with the vegetables. Rock the casserole from side to side to make sure everything is combined. Heat through very gently for a few minutes, stirring all the time. Adjust the seasoning and serve the slices of meat and vegetables in large bowls with the sauce spooned over the top.

30 g (1 oz) butter

2 tablespoons olive oil

800 g (1 lb 12 oz) piece of lean veal (topside or silverside)

3 garlic cloves, crushed

6 whole allspice (pimento) berries

1 bay leaf

1 litre (35 fl oz/4 cups) water

2 large potatoes, cut into chunks and kept in cold water

2 large carrots, cut into wedges

30 g (1 oz) plain (all-purpose) flour

juice of 1 lemon

125 ml (4 fl oz/½ cup) thin (pouring) cream

3 tablespoons chopped dill

# ROAST VEAL WITH ORANGES & LEMONS

There is not too much orange and lemon, just a hint, but I love the citrus wedges and a roasted thyme sprig served on the plate with the veal so that you know exactly what has gone into the cooking. (If you want, you can add more orange and lemon wedges towards the end of the cooking time, although they could make the sauce a little more tart.) The meat should be deep golden on the outside and cooked but just slightly rosy inside. You will need a small roasting dish (mine is about 25 x 18 cm/10 x 7 inches) that fits the meat and vegetables quite compactly and can transfer to the stovetop.

Preheat the oven to 200°C (400°F/Gas 6). Cut the whole orange and lemon into quarters lengthways (or into 6 wedges, if they are large) and put to one side. Keep the halves for later.

Put the oil and butter in a flameproof roasting tin and put over medium heat until the butter melts. Add the veal, garlic, shallots and carrots, turn the heat to high and brown the meat, salting and peppering the done sides and turning the vegetables over when you turn the meat.

Add the rosemary and thyme and put the tin in the oven. Roast for about 20 minutes, or until the surface of the veal looks bubbling and golden, then turn it over. Squeeze in the juice from the orange and lemon halves, and add the wine. Roast for 10 minutes, then add the orange and lemon wedges. Reduce the temperature to 180°C (350°F/Gas 4) and roast for another 10 minutes. Turn the wedges, taking care not to pierce them and ruin their shape, then roast for a final 20 minutes. Remove from the oven and let the dish sit for about 15 minutes.

Remove the string before carving the meat into fine slices. Serve with the pan juices, some carrots and an orange and lemon wedge for each person.

SERVES 4–5

1½ oranges

1½ lemons

3 tablespoons olive oil

30 g (1 oz) butter

about 700 g (1 lb 9 oz) veal nut, tied with string to keep its shape

2 garlic cloves, unpeeled

2 French shallots, peeled and halved lengthways

4 carrots, peeled and cut into thirds

2 rosemary sprigs

4 thyme sprigs

125 ml (4 fl oz/½ cup) white wine

# PREGO ROLLS & CHILLI OIL

I love prego rolls and actually crave them at times. The steaks should be just a couple of millimetres thick and the wine not too heavy. The best bread rolls to use are the floury rosette type. You have to have everything ready, as the meat will only take a couple of minutes to cook and these really need to be eaten warm. A teaspoonful of this chilli oil (and a bit of the chilli itself) can be drizzled on top, and can also be drizzled over pasta, skewers, grilled (broiled) meats and salads. The oil will initially be very hot, but as it is used you can top it up with more olive oil and it will eventually lose some of its potency. The flavour will depend entirely on your choice of chillies. Be sure to wear rubber gloves when handling the chillies, as just a little on your skin can prove uncomfortable even a few hours later (especially if you rub your eyes).

Marinate the meat in the wine, whole garlic cloves and rosemary for a couple of hours. Leave it covered in a cool place. If it is in the fridge, bring it back to room temperature before cooking.

Keep the marinade and pat the meat dry with paper towel. Heat a large non-stick frying pan to very hot and add 1 tablespoon of the olive oil. Fry the steaks quickly on both sides until cooked and lightly golden, sprinkling a little salt on the cooked side. Take care not to overcook and dry out the meat. Transfer the meat to a plate. Remove the rosemary sprig and quickly add the marinade to the pan with the butter. Return to the heat and cook until it bubbles up and thickens slightly.

Spoon some juice over the bottom half of each roll, top with a steak, drizzle over a little more juice and then dip the cut side of the roll top in the pan juice. Drizzle any remaining juice and about a tablespoon of olive oil over each steak. People can dress their rolls themselves with a bit of chopped chilli in oil (see below), salt and lemon juice.

To make the chilli oil (this is best made a few days, or even a week ahead of time) put the sliced chillies in a colander in the sink and remove as many of the seeds as you can by tapping the colander sharply on the side of the sink. Sprinkle generously with salt and put a plate that fits inside your colander on top of the chillies to squash them and extract some of the juice. Set aside for about 24 hours.

Using gloves, squeeze the chillies with your hands to drain away the excess salt and moisture and pack them into a clean sterilised jar. Cover them completely with the olive oil. The oil will be ready in a couple of days, but will be better in a couple of weeks. Add more olive oil if the chilli oil is too strong. Store in a cool place. The chillies must remain covered by the oil at all times.

## SERVES 2

2 soft rump steaks (about 120 g/ 4¼ oz each)

125 ml (4 fl oz/½ cup) red wine

2 large garlic cloves, lightly crushed with the flat of a knife

1 rosemary sprig

3 tablespoons olive oil

20 g (¾ oz) butter

2 floury bread rolls, halved

chopped chillies in oil, to serve (see below)

lemon wedges, to serve

## CHILLI OIL
### (MAKES 1 LARGE JAR)

about 40 fresh red chillies, cut into thin rounds of about 2 mm (1⁄16 inch)

salt

375 ml (13 fl oz/1½ cups) olive oil

# BEEF KEBABS WITH BAY LEAVES

These spiced grilled skewers are made with many different meats — chicken, fish, lamb — but the one I love most is beef fillet. You might like to spice it up a bit with some crushed herbs in the marinade. It's important to use fresh rather than dried bay leaves — they give a wonderful deep and special flavour. You'll need six or so metal or wooden skewers to make these, but when you serve it's not necessary for everyone to have their own skewer; it will depend on how large you cut the pieces of meat. I like this with roasted new potatoes and tomatoes.

Put the meat in a bowl and sprinkle with the paprika. Add 2 whole bay leaves, 3 squashed garlic cloves, the olive oil, some pepper and coarse salt. Turn it all through, massaging the salt into the meat. Cover, refrigerate and leave for a couple of hours. If you're using wooden skewers, put them in water to soak now, so they don't scorch on the barbecue.

Heat up your barbecue and, while it's warming, thread the meat and remaining bay leaves alternately onto skewers. Brush the bay leaves with a touch of oil to stop them burning. Put a rack fairly close over the hot barbecue (about 10 cm/4 inches away) and cook the skewers, turning often, until crusty golden and charred here and there but rosy inside.

Meanwhile, heat the butter with the last garlic clove in a small pan until it's a bit golden and smells good. Keep warm on the side of the barbecue if the skewers aren't yet ready.

Put the skewers on a platter, scatter immediately with a little more coarse salt and some pepper, drizzle with the warm butter and serve at once. The meat will be deliciously soft and tender and the juices will seep out and mingle with the butter.

MAKES 6 OR 7 'BIG PIECE' SKEWERS

about 900 g (2 lb) beef fillet, with some fat on, cut into 5 cm (2 inch) pieces

¾ teaspoon sweet paprika

about 20 or more fresh bay leaves

4 garlic cloves, peeled and squashed a bit

3 tablespoons olive oil

coarse salt

30 g (1 oz) butter

# 8

~ VEGETABLES & SIDES ~

# FRIED ZUCCHINI & AUBERGINE

A wonderful thing I learnt in Greece one summer was this quick twice-flouring and dipping in water method that produces a great crispy result. So have a bowl of flour and a bowl of cold water ready. It may seem like a bit of a fuss but it's worth it. This is a beauty with tzatziki for dipping the fried vegetables into.

Cut the zucchini into slices of about 3 mm (⅛ inch) thick. Cut the eggplant into half-moons of about 3 mm (⅛ inch) thick. Put the flour onto a plate, and have a bowl of cold water ready.

Pour the olive oil into a large non-stick frying pan to roughly 1 cm (½ inch) deep and heat. Pat slices of zucchini in flour to coat both sides. Shake off the excess then dip the slices in the water. Shake a bit and pat well in flour again on both sides. Fry in batches until golden, turning them over and frying the other side too. Don't overcrowd the pan and if they're cooking too quickly, then turn the heat down. Remove the crisp and golden zucchini slices to a large plate lined with paper towel. Mix the salt, pepper and oregano together then sprinkle over the fried vegetables and get the next batch going.

Once the zucchini are done, do the exact same thing with the eggplant. Serve hot, with tzatziki. These are also lovely with lemon.

SERVES 3

1 zucchini (courgette)
  (about 200 g/7 oz)
½ an eggplant (aubergine)
  (about 200 g/7 oz), halved
  lengthways
plain (all-purpose) flour, for coating
light olive oil, for frying
1 teaspoon salt
a few grinds of black pepper
2 teaspoons dried oregano
tzatziki (see page 241), to serve

# STUFFED VEGETABLES

This is a wonderful colourful tray of mixed vegetables, which you can vary according to what's easily available and in season (you could use only tomatoes or try mixed colours of peppers). These make a fantastic main course, and can be made in advance and served at room temperature or warmed up before serving if you prefer. I've used a combination of tomatoes, peppers and zucchini, which can be halved or divided, so that everyone gets a taste of each.

SERVES 6–8

Preheat the oven to 200°C (400°F/Gas 6). Put the meat in a large bowl with the onion, parsley, rice, 4 tablespoons of oil, paprika, mint, pepper and salt.

Slice the tops off the tomatoes and keep them on one side. Hollow out the insides of the tomatoes with a teaspoon (a pointed one is easiest), holding them over a bowl to catch the juice. Chop up the pulp and add to the meat with half of the juice from the tomatoes. Keep the rest of the juice. Sit the tomatoes in a large oven tray.

Cut away a top hat from each pepper, leaving a hinge of a couple of centimetres (¾ inch) on one side. Scoop out the seeds and throw them away, but save any of the fleshy pepper bits that you can. Chop up this flesh and add it to the meat. Put the peppers on the tray — it doesn't matter if they don't sit flat, they can lie down.

continues on next page …

900 g (2 lb) minced (ground) beef and pork

2 large red onions, finely grated

15 g (½ oz/½ cup) chopped flat-leaf parsley

250 g (9 oz) uncooked short-grain rice

4 tablespoons olive oil, plus 125 ml (4 fl oz/½ cup) extra

1 heaped teaspoon sweet paprika

1 teaspoon dried mint, crumbled

1 teaspoon ground black pepper

2 teaspoons salt

6–8 ripe tomatoes

4 peppers (capsicums)

4 zucchini (courgettes)

4 potatoes, cut in half lengthways and then into halves or thirds

3 tablespoons butter, melted

juice of ½ a lemon

Cut away a hat from each zucchini and scrape out the flesh with a pointed teaspoon. Chop this up and add it to the meat. Put the zucchini on the tray. (Or, cut the zucchini in half and scrape out a hollow from each side with a potato peeler or pointed spoon, so that you have the two hollowed-out halves, now upright.) Holding the meat bowl with one hand, mix thoroughly with your other hand, turning the meat filling from the bottom of the bowl up, so that it is all well combined. Fill the hollowed-out vegetables with the meat filling, using your hands or a tablespoon, until the mixture is flush with the tops. Don't overstuff them: wait and see that they have all been filled and then you can go back and add a bit more here and there. Add the potatoes around the vegetables.

Pour the remaining 125 ml (4 fl oz/½ cup) of oil into the remaining tomato juice and add the butter, lemon juice and 375 ml (13 fl oz/1½ cups) of water. Mix together and pour carefully over and around the vegetables. Put the tops back on the vegetables and sprinkle with salt, especially the potatoes.

Bake for about 1¼–1½ hours, until the vegetables are golden and darkened in places and seem soft even at the bottom. (If your vegetables dry out, add a little extra water, but this shouldn't be necessary.) These should not be served really hot: turn the oven off and leave them in there for at least 15 minutes before serving (they are best if you can manage to leave them in for a couple of hours). They are good at room temperature, or even the next day.

# TZATZIKI

This is a subtle amount of garlic compared with some versions that you may come across. So you can add more if you like. If the garlic bothers you, you can leave it out completely, but it's not really tzatziki then. (And, garlic is good for colds plus it keeps vampires away.)

Tzatziki is a beauty as it takes just about anything to a different level. Wonderful with chips, lamb chops, bread and many other dishes. You can use 2 teaspoons or so of dried mint instead of fresh. If you prefer a milder garlic taste, then marinate the garlic in the oil and pour off the oil after without adding the garlic. If you are making regular tzatziki, then just make sure everyone within a five-mile radius has some.

---

Using the flat of your knife, crush the garlic with a pinch of salt into a paste. Put into a small bowl with the oil and leave to marinate while you proceed with the rest.

Top and tail the cucumber, and peel it. I like it striped, with one strip peeled and the next left unpeeled. Using the large holes of a grater, grate the cucumber into a sieve. Scatter with the salt and leave it for 30 minutes or so to drain, turning it over a couple of times and even squashing it down with your hands or a wooden spoon.

Put the yoghurt into a bowl for serving. Add the garlic and oil, the mint and a couple of grinds of black pepper. Fold the cucumber through and taste for salt. This can be stored in the fridge, covered, for a couple of days. The cucumber will give up a little water but stir it through to loosen the tzatziki.

**MAKES A NICE BOWLFUL**

2 garlic cloves
1 tablespoon olive oil
1 small cucumber
    (about 160 g/5½ oz)
1 teaspoon salt
350 g (12 oz) Greek yoghurt
1½ tablespoons chopped mint

# ARTICHOKES
# & BROAD BEANS

This is a beautiful spring dish they serve in Greece. It can be served as a side dish or as a main with a plate of feta and some bread. Freshly podded peas are also lovely here if you prefer them to the broad beans. Drizzle a little extra virgin olive oil over to serve, and pepper.

SERVES 8

Pod the beans and take off their outer jackets (if they don't come off easily you can drop them in boiling water for a few seconds). The small very green beans can be left, as their jackets are not tough. Put the juice of 1½ lemons in a large bowl (non-metallic) of cold water. Snap the tough outer leaves off the artichokes and discard. You may need to remove more than you think before you get to the tender leaves. Slice off the hard top of the leaves, maybe even one-third of the top depending on the size and type of artichoke. Leave 4 cm (1½ inches) or so of stalk and cut off the rest. Using a potato peeler or small sharp knife, peel the stems and the base of the artichokes. Halve them from top to bottom then remove the choke with a small knife or pointed spoon. Put the cleaned artichokes immediately into the lemon water to prevent them from darkening.

Heat the oil in a large non-stick frying pan. Add the spring onion and gently sauté until pale gold. Drain the artichokes, pat them dry with paper towel and add them to the pan in a single layer. Cook, turning once, until slightly coloured. Season with salt and pepper, add 250 ml (9 fl oz/1 cup) of water, put the lid on and simmer for 10 minutes or until just tender and there is a little thickened sauce left in the pan. If there isn't much sauce left, add a little hot water. Add the broad beans, leave the lid off and cook for another few minutes. Sprinkle in the remaining lemon juice, dill and mint, rocking the pan for everything to mingle. Remove from the heat and leave for a few minutes before serving. This can also be served at room temperature, but is best warm.

The same ingredients are lovely served raw with extra virgin olive oil and a piece of cheese and bread. Simply shelled broad beans, cleaned artichokes, spring onions, fresh dill and mint leaves. Serve with ouzo on ice.

**1.5 kg (3 lb 5 oz) broad (fava) beans in their pods (250 g/9 oz podded and skinned)**

**juice of 2½ lemons**

**8 artichokes (about 220 g/7¾ oz each) with a stem of about 6 cm/ 2½ inches)**

**125 ml (4 fl oz/½ cup) olive oil**

**100 g (3½ oz) (about 3 large) round spring onions (scallions), trimmed and roughly chopped**

**2 tablespoons chopped dill**

**1 tablespoon roughly chopped mint**

# BEETROOT WITH YOGHURT & PISTACHIOS

This is the way my friend Annette makes her beetroot salad.
I love the colours here. And its freshness, even though it looks
mayonnaisey; it's a surprise to remember that it's actually much
lighter than it looks. This is wonderful with fresh, roasted beetroot,
or you can also use ready-cooked beetroots in which case it will
only take a second to put together. If you are using fresh ones and
they have leaves you can boil those too for a few minutes and dress
them with olive oil to serve. If using fresh, cut the leaves well above
the bulb so that they don't bleed.

SERVES 4–6

Preheat the oven to 180°C (350°F / Gas 4). Wash the beetroots well, being
careful not to pierce their skins. Cut off the leaves, leaving 2–3 cm (about
1¼ inches) attached so the beetroot doesn't bleed, and leave the root for
now. Wrap each beetroot individually in foil and bake for about 1 hour until
tender when tested with a sharp knife.

Whip the oil lightly in a bowl with the lemon juice and garlic.

Wearing kitchen gloves, peel the beetroot. Trim away the root and cut them
into nice chunks. If you are using ready-cooked beetroot, rinse if necessary
and trim away any tough end bits and cut into chunks. Put in a bowl. Add the
lemon oil and parsley and season with salt and pepper. Add the yoghurt and
mix all through gently. Scatter the pistachio nuts on top and serve.

650 g (1 lb 7 oz) beetroot (beets)
(about 4), trimmed or 500 g
(1 lb 2 oz) ready-cooked beetroot

3 tablespoons olive oil

juice of ½ a lemon

2 garlic cloves, finely chopped

3 tablespoons coarsely chopped
flat-leaf parsley

340 g (11¾ oz) Greek yoghurt

10 g (¼ oz) shelled pistachio nuts,
chopped

# BROAD BEANS WITH CHOURIÇO

This is lovely to make in the short season when we can get fresh broad beans. It can be quite a job on account of peeling the beans, but also rather relaxing. I like to peel away the outer jacket of each parboiled bean, even if it makes for extra work. The insides are a beautiful, brighter green and are added to the pan towards the end of the cooking so they keep their colour.

Rinse the shelled beans and put them (or the frozen beans) in a pan of lightly salted boiling water and boil for about 5 minutes. Drain and peel off the outer skins. Many of them will split in half but that's fine — they are still lovely and smooth and beautiful.

Heat the oil in a large non-stick frying pan and sauté the chopped sausage for a couple of minutes. Add the onion and cook, stirring, for a few more minutes until it is sticky and the sausage is brown.

Add the garlic and stir until you start to smell it, then add the wine and a couple of twists of pepper. Cook until the wine has evaporated a bit, then stir in the broad beans and cook for a couple of minutes over high heat so the flavours will mingle. There should be just a bit of sauce in the bottom of the pan.

Stir in the mint or coriander right at the end and add a splash of red wine vinegar. Check for seasoning and serve warm with grilled bread or just-boiled potatoes.

**SERVES 4–6**

500 g (1 lb 2 oz) shelled fresh (or frozen) broad (fava) beans (about 3 kg/6 lb 12 oz in their pods)

2 tablespoons olive oil

160 g (5½ oz) *chouriço* sausage, chopped

1 small red onion, chopped

2 garlic cloves, chopped

125 ml (4 fl oz/½ cup) white wine

6–8 mint or coriander (cilantro) leaves, torn

a splash of red wine vinegar

# STEWED GREEN BEANS IN TOMATO SAUCE

This is often served as a main course in Greece, with feta to mingle in with the sauce, and bread. Of course it's also great served next to a main course such as roast meat, or fish. I have also seen potatoes added to the stew.

SERVES 6 OR SO

Cut the tops off the green beans and string them if necessary. Rinse and drain, keeping them in your colander for now.

Heat the olive oil in a large non-stick pot and sauté the onion until softened and almost sticky. Add the garlic and, when you can smell it, add the tomatoes, parsley, 2–3 grinds of pepper and a good amount of salt. Simmer, uncovered, over medium heat for about 8 minutes, until the tomatoes soften and collapse. Add the beans and 250 ml (9 fl oz/1 cup) of hot water. Scatter the cinnamon over the beans and put the lid on. When it comes to the boil, turn the beans through then put the lid back on and simmer until the beans are soft, about 20 minutes, turning through a few times so that no lonely beans sit out of the sauce for long. At the end of this time there should be a good amount of thickish sauce. If you think it needs it, stir in a little water. Now turn off the heat and leave them for a while, covered, to absorb the flavours. Take the pot to the table and serve warm.

about 800 g (1 lb 12 oz) flat green beans

5 tablespoons olive oil

1 red onion, chopped

3 garlic cloves, chopped

400 g (14 oz) tinned chopped tomatoes

2 tablespoons roughly chopped flat-leaf parsley

¼ teaspoon ground cinnamon

# BAKED PUMPKIN WITH BUTTER & BROWN SUGAR

This is lovely and sweet and goes very well with roast pork or chicken, and also game if you happen to be serving that. I use organic pumpkin which is a beautiful reddish orange outside and butternut orange inside. Make sure you start off with a lovely pumpkin, but if you suspect yours is not very ripe and tasty, you could add a little more sugar. You might like to add another vegetable here too, like turnips or other root vegetables. You can also add some ground cinnamon before baking. I use a 32 cm (about 12½ inches) round baking dish, but you can work out how many you need to serve and what size dish will be right, as these are very easy amounts to adjust.

**SERVES 6**

50 g (1¾ oz) butter

about 1 kg (2 lb 4 oz) unpeeled pumpkin (winter squash)

50–70 g (1¾–2½ oz) light brown sugar

2 bay leaves

Preheat the oven to 180°C (350°F/Gas 4) and generously butter the bottom of a large round ovenproof dish with some of the butter. Peel the pumpkin by first cutting it in half, then scooping out the seeds with a spoon (save the seeds to toast in the oven for a snack, or to plant). Cut the pumpkin into long slices that are 2–3 cm (about 1¼ inches) thick. Using a small sharp knife, carefully cut away the skin, keeping the shape of the pumpkin slices and taking care that you don't cut yourself, as the skin is hard. You should have about 750 g (1 lb 10 oz) of pumpkin.

Scatter some of the sugar over the bottom of the dish and then lay the pumpkin slices flat, in a single layer. Scatter the rest of the sugar over the top, dot with the rest of the butter and sprinkle with a little salt. Pour 3 tablespoons of water around the side and add the bay leaves. Put into the oven for about 1 hour, or until the pumpkin is soft and golden, even dark in places, and there is some thick golden juice bubbling away at the bottom. Spoon the pan juices over the pumpkin a couple of times during the cooking — if it looks a little too dry, add a dribble more water. Serve warm. If you aren't serving it immediately, then reheat gently so that the butter melts again.

# ROASTED ZUCCHINI &
# TOMATOES WITH THYME

I love this — it is healthy and appetising; tasty for a side dish, or
as a light meal on its own with some bread. It is important that
your tomatoes are deep red and beautifully ripe. I particularly like
this simple combination, but you can use other herbs instead —
perhaps basil or rosemary — and you might like to include some
other vegetables, depending on who you are serving and what they
like. Red peppers (capsicums), eggplant (aubergines) and potatoes
could all be cut up and included here. You'll need one large baking
dish of about 35 x 25 cm (14 x 10 inches) where the vegetables can
sit quite flat. If you aren't going to serve this immediately, switch off
the oven when the vegetables are cooked, but leave the dish in there
to cool down completely.

SERVES 6–8

Preheat the oven to 200°C (400°F/Gas 6). Trim the zucchini and slice
them diagonally into chunks of about 3 cm (1¼ inches): slice once in one
direction, and then in the other direction, and so on. Put them in a large
baking dish. Slice the carrots diagonally in one direction to give longish strips
about 3 mm (⅛ inch) thick. Add to the dish. Cut the tomatoes into wedges
(six or eight depending on the size of the tomato) from top to bottom. Put in
the dish and add the garlic, celery, parsley and oil. Season quite generously
with salt and pepper, roll up your sleeves and mix everything through with
your hands. I love doing this, and so do my kids, but you can use a large
spoon if you prefer. Bury the thyme sprigs underneath and put the dish in the
oven. Bake, uncovered, for 30 minutes, turning the vegetables over once in
this time.

Turn the vegetables again, lower the heat to 180°C (350°F/Gas 4) and cook
for another 1¼ hours, or until the vegetables are golden roasted and moist
and the natural sweetness of the tomatoes and carrots has come into being.
Turn the vegetables once or twice more during this time, trying not to mash
things up, but the tomatoes will invariably be melting and losing their shape.
There should be very little liquid left, so you may have to add a few drops of
water. Serve hot, or at room temperature.

600 g (1 lb 5 oz) ( about 7 or 8 small)
zucchini (courgettes)

600 g (1 lb 5 oz) (about 3 or 4)
carrots, peeled

800 g (1 lb 12 oz)(about 6) tomatoes

3 garlic cloves, finely chopped

1 leafy celery stalk, halved
lengthways and thinly sliced

3 tablespoons chopped flat-leaf
parsley

6 tablespoons olive oil

6 thyme sprigs

# BAKED OKRA

*Bamies* (okra) are enjoyed in Greece when they are in season. They are often stewed on the stovetop but here they are baked, which I really like. Also called ladies' fingers, they are rather a particular vegetable, containing a glutinous substance that thickens dishes. They are great served with a dish of feta and some bread and perhaps a green salad. Try and get small okra of around 4 cm (1½ inches) in length, so there is less chance of tough or stringy ones. This dish is sometimes also baked with chicken pieces in it.

**SERVES 8 OR SO**

600 g (1 lb 5 oz) small okra

80 ml (2½ fl oz/⅓ cup) wine vinegar

1 tablespoon coarse salt

6 tablespoons olive oil

1 large red onion, chopped

2 small green sweet peppers (capsicums) (about 60 g/2¼ oz each), halved lengthways, seeded and sliced

2 garlic cloves, finely chopped

400 g (14 oz) tinned chopped tomatoes

2 tablespoons chopped flat-leaf parsley

Rinse and drain the okra. Trim the top of their hard stems in a circular conical way so that the top isn't pierced and no seeds can leak out. Put them into a bowl of cold water with the vinegar and salt and leave for an hour or so. Drain into a colander and rinse well.

Preheat the oven to 180°C (350°F/Gas 4). Heat the olive oil in a non-stick frying pan and sauté the onion until soft and sticky. Add the peppers towards the end, sauté for a couple of minutes, then add the garlic. When you can smell it frying, add the tomatoes. Simmer for about 5 minutes, mashing any tomato lumps with a wooden spoon. Stir in 500 ml (17 fl oz /2 cups) of water and the parsley, and season with salt and pepper. Add the okra, gently turning them to coat well.

Turn out into a 30 x 22 cm (12 x 8½ inch) baking dish and bake uncovered for about 50 minutes. Gently turn the okra over and continue baking until the okra are roasted looking and the sauce is thick and dark and no longer watery, about 30 minutes. If it seems like the okra are getting too dark too quickly, turn the oven down slightly. Taste one to see if it is lovely and soft. Cool a little before serving to allow the okra to absorb the juices.

# ROAST PUMPKIN &
# MUSHROOMS

This is so simple and lovely. You can make it ahead of time and pop it into a hot oven to reheat for a moment just before serving. I tend to use my round 30 cm (12 inch) baking dish to make this but you could use a rectangular one of about 26 x 23 cm (10½ x 9 inches) and about 5 cm (2 inches) deep. You can easily add more pumpkin and mushrooms here — just fill up your dish.

Preheat your oven to 180°C (350°F/Gas 4). Peel the pumpkin, remove the seeds and cut the flesh into 5 mm (¼ inch) slices. You should have about 600 g (1 lb 5 oz) pumpkin slices.

Drizzle some of the olive oil into your baking dish. Add the pumpkin slices, mushrooms, garlic and rosemary and season with salt and pepper, then drizzle over the rest of the olive oil. Turn well using your hands or a wooden spoon, then spread everything out more or less rustically.

Bake for 30–40 minutes until the pumpkin is tender and golden in places and the mushrooms are crisp and golden here and there. Scatter with parmesan and bake for another 5–10 minutes. Serve warm or even at room temperature.

SERVES 4–6

800 g (1 lb 12 oz) pumpkin
    (winter squash)
5 tablespoons olive oil
about 400 g (14 oz) fresh porcini,
    field or Swiss brown mushrooms,
    cut into chunks
2 garlic cloves, chopped
1 tablespoon finely chopped
    rosemary
about 3 tablespoons grated parmesan
    cheese

# PUMPKIN PIZZA

This is not really a pizza, but it looks like one. It is very important to make the pumpkin slices as thin and long as you can, and you can keep the seeds, rinse them and bake them in the oven to serve as a snack with a sprinkling of salt. Next time you make this you could even try adding a few dollops of leftover cooked minced (ground) meat between the layers of pumpkin.

Peel the pumpkin, cut out the seeds and cut the flesh into very thin, long slices about 2 mm (1/16 inch) thick. Put the slices in a colander, sprinkle with salt and leave for about 1 hour. Rinse them very well and pat dry. Preheat the oven to 180°C (350°F/Gas 4).

Drizzle 2 tablespoons of the olive oil into a round 25–30 cm (10–12 inch) baking dish and spread it to coat the base of the dish. Put the flour on a plate and pat both sides of the pumpkin slices in it. Make a slightly overlapping layer of slices in the baking dish. Trickle the tiniest bit of olive oil over this layer, then repeat the layering and oiling until you have used up all the pumpkin (you should have four or five layers).

Mix a little salt into the passata and dot here and there over the top of the pumpkin. Put the dish into the oven and bake for about 50 minutes, until the bottom is sizzling and the top is turning quite golden. Scatter the oregano over the top, crushing it between your fingers. Sprinkle with the mozzarella and return to the oven for 5–10 minutes, until the cheese melts and browns slightly. Cool a little before serving in wedges like pizza.

**SERVES 6**

about 1.4 kg (3 lb 2 oz/½ a small) pumpkin (winter squash)

4–6 tablespoons olive oil

about 125 g (4½ oz) plain (all-purpose) flour, for dusting

200 ml (7 fl oz) tomato passata (puréed tomatoes)

1–2 teaspoons dried oregano

125 g (4½ oz) mozzarella cheese, grated

# 9

~ DESSERTS ~

# PEAR & BERRY CRUMBLE

You can use any ripe sweet fruit you like for this, really — peaches, apples, apricots, nectarines, pineapples … This is best served warm, when it has cooled down a bit, with a jug of warm custard or just a blob of thick or clotted cream on the side, and a dusting of icing (confectioners') sugar. Sometimes I like the crumble topping to be soft, soft, and then I use 60 g (2¼ oz) of icing sugar instead of the brown sugar and caster sugar. If you feel your fruit might not be sweet enough, sprinkle a dash more sugar over it before the crumble topping goes on. You can mix some chopped shelled walnuts (about 30 g/1 oz) through the topping for a nutty crunch.

**SERVES 8**

Preheat your oven to 190°C (375°F/Gas 5). Generously butter a 36 x 22 x 6 cm (14¼ x 8½ x 2½ inch) ovenproof dish. Peel, core and slice the pears and put them in the dish. Mix in the berries and scatter half the caster sugar over the fruit.

Mix together the flour, brown sugar and the other half of the caster sugar in a bowl. Add the butter and vanilla and rub them in with your fingertips, working until the mixture isn't smooth but looks like damp clustery sand. Your fingers might be tired.

Scatter the topping over the fruit to cover it completely in a good thick layer. Bake for about 45 minutes, or until the top is nicely golden and some berry juice has oozed up a bit over the crust and darkened it here and there.

Let it cool down a touch and then serve warm with whipped thick or clotted cream, a jug of custard or vanilla ice cream.

1 kg (2 lb 4 oz) pears
1 cup of mixed berries (about 200 g/ 7 oz depending on the berries)
70 g (2½ oz) caster (superfine) sugar
200 g (7 oz) plain (all-purpose) flour
50 g (1¾ oz) light brown sugar
150 g (5½ oz) butter, softened
1 teaspoon vanilla extract

# BANANA BREAD

This is my schoolfriend Alexia's recipe: her mum is a fantastic cook and she always made this. It is a healthy snack or breakfast and an excellent way to use up bananas that otherwise might be on their way out. I always end up making this because bananas in my house just never keep the pale waxy complexion that they have in the shops. For some reason they start deteriorating the minute they come home with me. You can add some chopped walnuts or hazelnuts, too, and some cinnamon. Serve it on its own, or even lightly buttered and with your favourite jam.

Preheat the oven to 180°C (350°F/Gas 4) and butter a 30 x 11 cm (12 x 4¼ inch) loaf (bar) tin.

Cream the butter and sugar until smooth and then whisk in the mashed bananas. Add the eggs, vanilla, cinnamon and a pinch of salt and whisk in well. Sift in the flour and baking powder and beat until smooth. Mix the bicarbonate of soda into the milk and stir into the batter.

Scrape the mixture into the tin and bake for about 50 minutes, until the bread is crusty on the top and a skewer poked into the middle comes out clean. Turn out onto a rack to cool.

Serve warm or cold, plain or toasted with butter, but allow to cool completely before storing in an airtight container, where it will keep well for several days.

**CUTS INTO 10–12 SLICES**

125 g (4½ oz) butter

180 g (6½ oz/1 cup) dark brown sugar

350 g (12 oz/3 or 4 medium) ripe bananas, mashed

2 eggs

1 teaspoon vanilla extract

1 teaspoon ground cinnamon

250 g (9 oz) plain (all-purpose) flour

1 teaspoon baking powder

¾ teaspoon bicarbonate of soda (baking soda)

3 tablespoons warm milk

# CHOCOLATE & VANILLA BISCUITS

These are lovely and easy, and something that kids can make from beginning to end, as long as you don't worry too much how they turn out. They could also be good to use for making and shaping Christmas decorations — you could make white or brown faces with eyes, mouth, hair, even white and brown plaits ... You might like to add some ground cinnamon, anise, cardamom or other spices to the dough.

Mash together the butter and sugar in a bowl with a wooden spoon. Add a pinch of salt and all but 20 g (¾ oz) of the flour and work them in. Whisk the egg with the vanilla and add this to the bowl, mixing it all well. Now knead it quickly, gently and thoroughly. Divide the dough in half. Add the cocoa to one half, kneading it in thoroughly. Knead the remaining 20 g (¾ oz) of flour into the other half. Pat both doughs down into flattish discs, cover separately with plastic wrap and refrigerate for about 30 minutes.

Preheat the oven to 180°C (350°F/Gas 4).

On a lightly floured surface, roll out the doughs separately to a thickness of about a few millimetres, depending on what you decide to make. You can cut out circles, squares and Christmas shapes with a biscuit cutter, cut free-form shapes with a small blunt knife, or make plaits by folding strips of each colour over each other and pressing the ends together. Put on baking trays lined with baking paper, allowing a little room for the biscuits to spread. Bake for 12–15 minutes, or until they are crisp.

**MAKES PLENTY!**

180 g (6½ oz) butter, softened

150 g (5½ oz) caster (superfine) sugar

1 egg

1 teaspoon vanilla extract

240 g (8¾ oz) plain (all-purpose) flour

20 g (¾ oz) unsweetened cocoa powder

# LEMON SANDWICHES WITH RASPBERRIES & CREAM

This basic lemon cake is very good on its own, fresh from the oven. But for something special, or to use the leftover cake, you can make these little sandwiches and serve them with coffee, or at an afternoon party. I use fresh raspberries and cream in these ones but you could use raspberry or strawberry jam and cream. The sandwiches are easier to cut when the cake is a day old.

Preheat the oven to 170°C (325°F/Gas 3) and butter and flour a 30 x 11 cm (12 x 4¼ inch) loaf (bar) tin.

Cream together the butter and sugar until light and fluffy. Beat in the eggs one by one. Sift in the flour and baking powder, then add the lemon zest, lemon juice, cream and vanilla. Whisk well to get a smooth batter.

Spoon into the loaf tin and bake for about 1 hour and 10 minutes, or until a skewer poked into the centre comes out clean. If the top looks like it's getting too brown before the cooking time is up, cover it with foil. Remove and leave to cool completely in the tin.

For the filling, whip the cream and icing sugar together until the cream holds peaks, then fold the yoghurt through. Cut the cake like a loaf of bread into slices about 5 mm (¼ inch) thick. Spread half the slices with cream, and then top with the raspberries and the rest of the cake slices to make sandwiches. Dust with icing sugar to serve.

**MAKES ABOUT 20 SANDWICHES**

250 g (9 oz) butter, softened

280 g (10 oz) caster (superfine) sugar

3 eggs

310 g (11 oz) plain (all-purpose) flour

1½ teaspoons baking powder

finely grated zest and juice of 1 lemon

185 ml (6 fl oz/¾ cup) thin (pouring) cream

1 teaspoon vanilla extract

**FILLING**

100 ml (3½ fl oz) whipping cream

2 teaspoons icing (confectioners') sugar, plus extra for dusting

100 g (3½ oz) Greek-style natural yoghurt

100 g (3½ oz) raspberries, halved

# ROSE DELIGHT

These are called *loukoumia*, and are most well known as Turkish delight. They are the sweets you are offered when you stop in at someone's even just for a quick visit. They are served with a glass of cold water. *Loukoumia* are also beautiful cut up into very small squares and served next to a coffee. The Greek island of Syros is well known for their *loukoumi*. They are often flavoured with rose, *mastiha* or pistachio. A sugar thermometer is important here to tell you when the sugar syrup is at the right stage.

Put the sugar and lemon juice in a pan with 185 ml (6 fl oz/¾ cup) of water. Stir until the sugar dissolves. Bring to the boil. Simmer without stirring for 30–40 minutes, or until a small dab is soft and pliable between your fingers when it's dropped into cold water (soft ball stage or 116°C/240°F on a sugar thermometer).

Combine the cornflour and cream of tartar in a heavy-based saucepan and whisk in 375 ml (13 fl oz /1½ cups) of water until smooth. Cook on medium, stirring constantly, until thick. Slowly stir in the sugar syrup. Simmer over very low heat (or use a simmer mat) until very thick and pale golden, 60–70 minutes. Stir often to ensure that your mixture isn't sticking to the pan. Brush a 21 x 12 cm (8¼ x 4½ inch) dish with straight sides with oil and line with plastic wrap. Stir the rosewater and pistachios into the mixture and add the colouring drop by drop until you have a soft rose-petal pink. Pour into the dish and cool overnight, covered by a cake net.

Combine the icing sugar and extra cornflour on a plate. Cut the *loukoumi* into 3 cm (1¼ inch) squares and toss in the sugar mix. It will keep for weeks in a covered tin or box, not an airtight container.

**MAKES 28 PIECES**

440 g (15½ oz/2 cups) sugar

1 teaspoon lemon juice

60 g (2¼ oz/½ cup) cornflour (cornstarch), plus 2 tablespoons extra for coating

½ teaspoon cream of tartar

2 teaspoons rosewater

20 g (¾ oz) shelled pistachios, halved lengthways

red food colouring

30 g (1 oz/¼ cup) icing (confectioners') sugar, for coating

2 tablespoons cornflour, extra for coating

# HAZELNUT CHOCOLATE BALLS

My kids absolutely loved to help me roll these in their small sweet palms when they were little — although it was difficult for them to try not to lick all the mixture off their hands. These are from a colleague of Giovanni's, my husband — he tasted them at work and spoke about them in such very descriptive terms that I made him hound her until she finally gave me the recipe.

MAKES ABOUT 30

Crumble the biscuits into a bowl and add the hazelnuts and about two-thirds of the hazelnut spread to start with. Mix together until it all looks a bit like mud cake. Try rolling a small portion into a ball — if it breaks up, mix in more chocolate hazelnut spread until it will hold a shape. If the weather is hot, put the mixture into the fridge for a while before rolling.

Line a tray or large flat plate with foil. Roll slightly heaped teaspoonfuls of mixture between your cool palms into compact little balls. Put them on the tray and into the fridge for an hour or so to firm up.

Melt the chocolate in the top of a double boiler, making sure that the water doesn't touch the top bowl. Remove from the heat and let the chocolate cool for a few minutes. Drop the balls in one by one, turning them around so that they are completely covered. Return them to the tray, where they will flatten a bit on the bottom. Let them set completely, even in the fridge for the first half hour or so if the weather's hot. Bring them out to room temperature and store in a tin in a cool dark place (or in the fridge in hot weather). They will keep for a couple of weeks.

3 hazelnut wafer biscuits

250 g (9 oz) roasted peeled hazelnuts, chopped quite finely

about 185 g (6½ oz) chocolate hazelnut spread

250 g (9 oz) dark (semi-sweet) chocolate

# LEMON RICE PUDDING WITH ROASTED PEACHES

My friend Jo — a wonderful cook — gave me this. You can use nectarines, if you prefer them to peaches, and it is also nice with plums. If you have any rice pudding left over, whisk an egg white into it, shape it into little balls and pan-fry them in butter. Sprinkle them with a little sugar and serve warm.

SERVES 6

Preheat the oven to its highest temperature. Heat the olive oil in a heavy-based pan, add the rice and stir gently to warm it. Add the milk, cream, lemon zest, vanilla bean and nutmeg and bring to the boil. Lower the heat and simmer steadily for about 10 minutes, stirring quite often to make sure it doesn't stick. Add the caster sugar and simmer for another 10 minutes, stirring as before. Meanwhile, toss the pistachios with a dash of the brown sugar in a small tray and roast in the oven until they are just crisp in places.

Put the peaches in a baking dish, cut side up. Scatter about ½ tablespoon of brown sugar over each peach half and top with a small blob of butter. Roast without turning until the tops are golden brown and the peaches are still in shape but with some juices bubbling.

Just as the rice is tender and creamy, but with quite a bit of milky liquid left, remove it from the heat and dish up into flat bowls. Serve with one or two peach halves with a little juice drizzled here and there and a small pile of sugared pistachios. This is good warm or cold.

2 tablespoons olive oil

200 g (7 oz) short-grain rice

1.25 litres (44 fl oz/5 cups) milk

250 ml (9 fl oz/1 cup) thin (pouring) cream

1 teaspoon finely grated lemon zest

½ a vanilla bean, split in half lengthways

freshly grated nutmeg

50 g (1¾ oz) caster (superfine) sugar, plus a little extra for the pistachios

60 g (2¼ oz) pistachios, skins removed

soft dark brown sugar, for sprinkling

3 peaches, stones removed, halved

6 small blobs of butter

# SPICED SYRUP CAKES

*Melomakarona* are small cakes drenched in honey syrup, which shout 'Christmas' in Greece. Take them as gifts in a box, or eat them slowly throughout the season. You can make them smaller if you like, even half this size (which are truly lovely).

Preheat the oven to 180°C (350°F / Gas 4) and line a baking tray with baking paper. Stir the sugar and oil in a wide bowl until the sugar dissolves. Add the brandy, orange juice and zest. Mix the baking powder, bicarbonate of soda, ground cinnamon, ground cloves and nutmeg through the flour. Add to the bowl and mix to a loose dough with a wooden spoon. Using your hands, knead to a soft and smooth dough.

Break off small clumps of dough of about 40 g (1½ oz) each (you should get 15). Roll them into a ball between your palms then form small oval shapes of about 6 x 4 cm (2½ x 1½ inches). Set them on the baking tray and bake until firm and the bases are golden, about 30 minutes.

While they are baking, make the syrup. Put all the ingredients along with 185 ml (6 fl oz / ¾ cup) of water in a small pot and stir over medium heat until the sugar dissolves. Simmer for 5 minutes, then keep warm.

Put the cakes in a dish with sides where they will fit in one layer. Stud each with a clove. Pour the syrup over them, covering each well. Leave them for 5 minutes. Spoon some syrup (it will be a little thicker now) from the bottom of the dish over the tops of the cakes and sprinkle with the walnuts. Remove to a serving plate. Drizzle the walnuts with remaining syrup. Cover with a cake net and cool completely. These will keep for many days, stored in a covered container.

MAKES 15

70 g (2 ½ oz) sugar

185 ml (6 fl oz / ¾ cup) extra virgin olive oil

3 tablespoons brandy

juice of ½ an orange

1 teaspoon grated orange zest

1 teaspoon baking powder

½ teaspoon bicarbonate of soda (baking soda)

2 teaspoons ground cinnamon

¼ teaspoon ground cloves

¼ teaspoon freshly grated nutmeg

300 g (10½ oz / 2 cups) plain (all-purpose) flour

15 whole cloves

20 g (¾ oz) crushed walnuts, to serve

SYRUP

175 g (6 oz / ½ cup) honey

140 g (5 oz) sugar

1 strip of orange zest

1 small cinnamon roll

# PASSIONFRUIT CRÈME CARAMEL

The island of San Miguel in the Azores, with its passionfruit and passionfruit liqueur, has many versions of this pudding. This is a dash lighter than the ones I ate in San Miguel, where less milk and more eggs seemed to be used. You will need an ample high ring tin here, please.

SERVES ABOUT 8

**CARAMEL**

200 g (7 oz) caster (superfine) sugar

1 tablespoon *maracuja* (passionfruit) liqueur or brandy

750 ml (26 fl oz/3 cups) milk

400 ml (14 fl oz) tinned condensed milk

7 eggs, lightly beaten

115 g (4 oz) caster (superfine) sugar

1 teaspoon vanilla extract

pulp from 8 passionfruit (about 150 ml/5 fl oz)

To make the caramel, tip the sugar into a heavy-based non-stick pan over medium heat and add a couple of tablespoons of water. Heat it up, stirring, until the sugar starts to melt, brushing down the side of the pan with a wet pastry brush to stop the sugar re-forming on the side. Once the sugar has melted, turn up the heat and stop stirring or it will crystallise. Let it bubble until deep golden brown, tilting the pan if you need to mix it together. Stir in the liqueur (watch for it spitting). Pour into a ring (bundt) tin, swirling so the caramel covers the bottom. Put the tin in a large roasting tin. Leave to cool while you make the filling.

Preheat your oven to 160°C (315°F/Gas 2–3). Heat the milk in a saucepan just to boiling point, then whisk in the condensed milk. Whisk the eggs, sugar and vanilla together very lightly — just enough to incorporate the sugar but not enough to make it froth. Add a ladleful of hot milk to the eggs, whipping to acclimatise them, then another ladleful, then pour in all the hot milk and whisk briefly. Stir in the passionfruit pulp.

Pour over the caramel in the tin (if you find it easier, pour it all into a jug and then into the ring tin). The custard will come right to the top. Pour boiling water into the roasting tin to come halfway up the side of the ring tin and lift very carefully into the oven. Bake for 1 hour or until the custard is set.

Leave to cool, then cover with plastic wrap and put in the fridge. This is best eaten the next day when the caramel has dissolved a bit and the custard has firmed up. To turn out, hold a plate firmly over the top of the tin, then flip over quickly, making sure it's landed squarely on the plate before you lift away the tin. Take care not to spill the sauce.

# PAVLOVAS WITH ORANGES & CHERRIES

This makes eight small pavlovas, but if you want one big one, just double the amounts and extend the cooking time by 10 minutes. The egg yolks can be used for making custard. If you are making a large pavlova, pile all the meringue into the centre of your lined baking tray and pat it out to about a 28 cm (11¼ inch) circle, smoothing the middle of the top where your cream and fruit will sit. If you want to make sixteen small pavlovas, use two baking trays and switch them around in the oven halfway through the baking time. And, if you want to, you can make them even smaller for children and get more out of the mixture. I like this with oranges and cherries but you can put pretty much any fruit on top with the cream. A few chopped pistachios always look good, as well.

Preheat the oven to 150°C (300°F/Gas 2) and line a large baking tray with baking paper. Whisk the egg whites in a large bowl and, once they form white peaks and start stiffening, add the cornflour. Begin adding the sugar, sprinkling it in a bit at a time, and keep whisking until you have added it all and everything seems like it may climb out of the bowl on its own. Whisk in the vanilla and vinegar.

Use two tablespoons to form the meringues on the baking tray — make eight rounded piles that are about 10 cm (4 inches) across, although you could make them a bit taller, slimmer or more elegant if you like. Flatten the tops slightly, so that your cream and fruit will have somewhere to sit, and smooth around the sides with the back of a teaspoon. Cook on the middle shelf of the oven for 40 minutes or so (check after 10 minutes and lower the temperature a little if the meringues are colouring). Switch off the oven and leave the pavlovas in for 30–40 minutes to cool, then remove them from the oven to cool completely. You can then store them in a tin at room temperature for up to 5 days until you are ready to serve them.

To serve, peel the oranges with a sharp knife, taking off all the pith. Cut out the segments by slicing down either side of the membranes. Halve the cherries and remove the stones. Whip the cream and icing sugar until peaks form, spoon onto the pavlovas and scatter with cherries and oranges. Dust with icing sugar to serve.

**SERVES 8**

3 large egg whites, at room temperature

1 teaspoon cornflour (cornstarch)

230 g (8 oz) caster (superfine) sugar

a few drops of vanilla extract

½ teaspoon apple or white wine cider

**TO SERVE**

2 oranges

24 cherries

250 ml (9 fl oz/1 cup) whipping cream

1 tablespoon icing (confectioners') sugar, plus extra for serving

# WATERMELON &
# ROSE PETAL JAM WITH
# BUTTERMILK PUDDING

As far as I am concerned, roses in food are the epitome of gorgeous. If you want to make this jam more rosy, add a few drops of rosewater, and if you have any petals left over you can always scatter them in your bath. This jam is quite runny and has a beautiful colour — it would be wonderful dribbled over a not-too-sweet ice cream or served with a blob of crème fraîche. If you can manage it, make the jam with the first of the watermelons and the last of the roses. If you prefer your jam thicker, cook half a chopped apple with the watermelon. You may need more or less sugar, depending on the sweetness of your watermelon. The buttermilk pudding would also be lovely served with some other fruit — perhaps syrupy poached quinces or a mixed berry salad. I like to use smooth pudding saucepans here, but you can use any ramekins you like. You can even serve the pudding in its ramekin with a little bowl of jam on the side.

To make the jam, put the watermelon in a bowl and sprinkle with the sugar. Halve the lemon and cut 3 thin slices from one half. Cut these slices into 8 pieces each and add to the bowl. Juice the remaining lemon and add to the bowl. Cover with plastic wrap and leave in the fridge overnight.

Pour the sugary fruit into a heavy-based saucepan suitable for making jam and bring to the boil. Lower the heat and simmer uncovered for about 1 hour, stirring frequently with a wooden spoon so that it doesn't stick. Ten minutes or so before you think it will be ready, remove half of the jam to a blender (making sure there are no lemon pieces included because those are nice left whole) and leave the rest of the jam to continue cooking. Purée this half and return it to the pan. (A few bits of watermelon and lemon give the jam a nice texture.)

continues on next page …

MAKES 625 ML (21½ FL OZ/2½ CUPS)
JAM AND 4 PUDDINGS

**JAM**

1 kg (2 lb 4 oz) ripe watermelon flesh (about 1.8 kg/4 lb watermelon with peel)

400 g (14 oz) caster (superfine) sugar

1 lemon

1 gorgeous untreated rose, petals separated and rinse

continues on next page …

To test if your jam is ready, spoon a little onto a plate and tilt it. It should slide down with resistance rather than just running down. If necessary, cook for longer. Add the rose petals and pour into a suitable sterilised jar, using a wide-necked funnel if necessary. Seal the jar tightly and turn over. Leave it to cool completely before turning the jar upright and storing in a cool place. Once opened, keep in the refrigerator and use up fairly quickly.

To make the puddings, soak the gelatine leaves in a bowl with enough cold water to cover them (you can snap the leaves of gelatine). If using powder, put 2 tablespoons of water in a glass bowl and sprinkle the gelatine evenly over the top. Leave to sponge and swell.

Put the cream, sugar and vanilla in a saucepan over medium heat to dissolve the sugar, then remove from the heat. Thoroughly squeeze out the softened gelatine leaves with your hands until they are like a ball of jelly. Add the gelatine leaves or the spongy gelatine to the warm cream and stir to dissolve it. Leave the mixture to cool, stirring from time to time to ensure the gelatine dissolves evenly. When completely cooled, stir in the buttermilk and strain through a sieve to remove any lumps of gelatine. Ladle into four 170 ml (5½ fl oz/⅔ cup) capacity ramekins. Put these on a tray, cover lightly with plastic wrap and put them in the fridge for at least a couple of hours before serving.

To serve, gently loosen around the sides of the puddings with your fingers or the back of a teaspoon. Dip the bottoms of the ramekins in a little hot water for a couple of seconds (no longer, or you'll end up with soup) and turn them out. Or, simply scoop out with a large spoon and pour some jam over the top before serving.

**BUTTERMILK PUDDING**
4 gelatine leaves (less than 2 g each)
  or 2 teaspoons gelatine powder
250 ml (9 fl oz/1 cup) thin (pouring)
  cream
100 g (3½ oz) caster (superfine)
  sugar
a few drops of vanilla extract
450 ml (16 fl oz) buttermilk

# SMALL BAKLAVA

These are my favourite baklava. Individual small ones packed row by row into a large tray. It's quite easy and totally worth it when you get your head around the maths. It may even give you a wonderful sense of achievement when they come out of the oven. The dish size, 30 x 26 cm (12 x 10½ inches) with straight sides, is important to give you eight rows of seven baklava — fifty-six baklava. If your dish size is different, you may have to adjust the amount of baklava for a packed-in result full of rows and rows of baklava. Also, the dimensions and weight of commercial filo varies from brand to brand and so you might need some additional maths to work out the number of sheets to use.

To make the syrup, stir the sugar and honey with 275 ml (9½ fl oz) of water in a saucepan until the sugar dissolves, then bring to the boil. Simmer for about 10 minutes or until slightly thickened. Cool.

Preheat the oven to 180°C (350°F / Gas 4). Melt the butter in a small saucepan until pale golden and smelling great. Cover the filo sheets with a clean dry cloth to stop them drying out while you work. Spread one sheet of filo on your work surface. Brush gently but well and generously all over with butter. Cover with the next sheet of filo, brush with butter and continue in this way until you have a stack of six sheets. Using a ruler and a sharp knife, measure and cut 7 cm (2¾ inch) squares. Fill and form this batch before buttering the next so that the filo won't dry.

Working quickly, drop about 4 pistachios into the centre of each square. Bring the four sides together to form a boat, then pinch them together at about two-thirds of the way up so the points of the filo open out like petals. Don't squash the top leaves together as their layerings are important for look and taste. Make sure that the bases are kept as square as possible, and they should measure about 3 cm (1¼ inches) square.

**continues on next page …**

---

**MAKES 56**

about 170 g (6 oz) butter

about 550 g (1 lb 4 oz) filo pastry (about 12 sheets of 48 x 37 cm / 19 x 14½ inches)

200 g (7 oz) shelled unsalted pistachio nuts

**SYRUP**
180 g (6½ oz) sugar

4½ tablespoons mild runny honey

Brush the base and sides of a 30 x 26 cm (12 x 10½ inch) ovenproof dish with melted butter. Line up the baklava in neat compact rows like bon-bons in a chocolate box. Repeat the full procedure with another 6 sheets of filo and continue until you have made 56 baklava. If you are respecting the measures given here, you may need to fold and cut a single filo sheet to make up the last few. Flick a little cold water over them with your fingers. Bake for 25–30 minutes until crisp and pale golden.

Drizzle half the syrup evenly over the hot baklava in long thin drizzles. Chop the remaining pistachios finely and scatter some over each baklava. Drizzle over the rest of the syrup to hold the nuts in place. Cool before serving. Keep, unrefrigerated, in the dish in which they're made covered by a cake net, or in a leakproof cake box of the type that you'd get from a baker's shop.

# OUZO SORBET

This is like a soft snow, sweet and ouzo-y and it works well after a meal — like an after-dinner mint.

SERVES 6–8

Stir the sugar into 750 ml (26 fl oz/3 cups) of water and bring to the boil. Simmer for 5 minutes. Cool. Stir in the ouzo and transfer to an ice-cream machine. Freeze following the manufacturer's instructions. Alternatively, pour it into a shallow tray and put in the freezer, breaking it up and beating with a fork three or four times before it becomes solid.

**220 g (7¾ oz/1 cup) sugar**
**7 tablespoons ouzo**

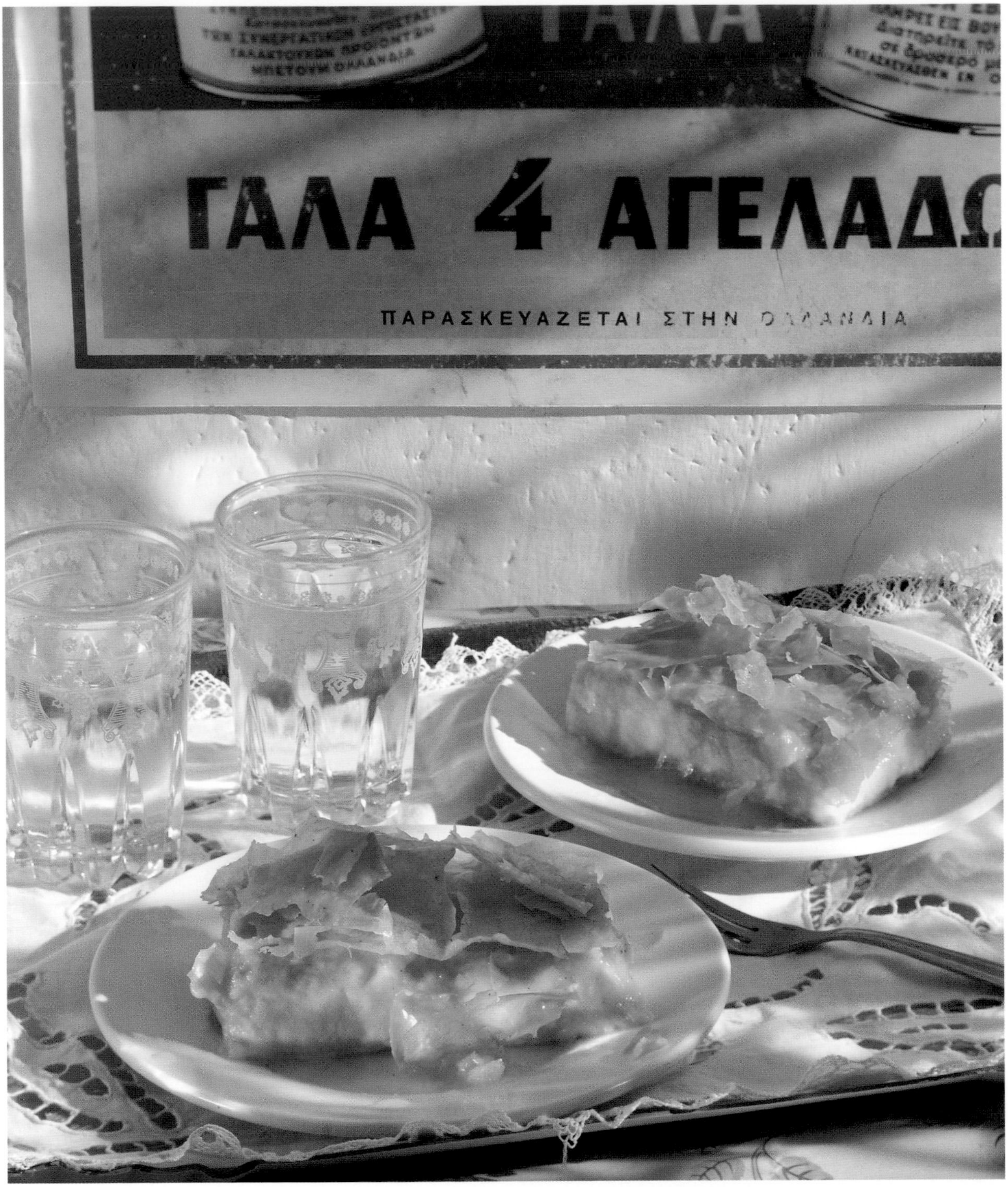
ΓΑΛΑ 4 ΑΓΕΛΑΔ
ΠΑΡΑΣΚΕΥΑΖΕΤΑΙ ΣΤΗΝ

# CUSTARD FILO PIE

This is my friend Annette's recipe. She is very good with desserts. I love the pureness of this pie. Syrupy Greek sweets are always served with a glass of cold water. Greeks have always loved making an outing to a café to have a sweet. This is often the type of sweet you will find served after Easter lamb.

SERVES 12

The butter should be heated and melted to a nice golden caramelly colour for good flavour, and while you are making this, you will probably have to put the butter back onto the stove to melt again when it hardens a bit.

To make the syrup, put the sugar and lemon peel in a small saucepan and add 185 ml (6 fl oz/¾ cup) of water. Put over medium heat and stir until the sugar dissolves. Bring to the boil and simmer for about 5 minutes. Remove from the heat and cool. Preheat the oven to 170°C (325°F/Gas 3).

For the filling put the sugar, semolina and cornflour in the bowl of an electric mixer. Add all the eggs and beat until thick and pale. Heat the milk, vanilla and nutmeg in a large saucepan to just below boiling. Add a ladleful to the eggs and mix in. Add another ladleful, mix, and continue until all the milk has been added. Scrape back into the pot and return it to the heat on low for 5–10 minutes, whisking often until it is very thick and nothing sticks to the bottom. When it's thickened and glooping and is just at the point before boiling, remove from the heat.

Have the filo sheets ready, covered by a tea towel to prevent them drying out. Brush the base and sides of a 30 x 22 cm (12 x 8½ inch) ovenproof dish with butter. Lay 1 sheet of filo on your work surface and brush it with butter. Cover with another sheet, brush it with butter and continue in this way until you have a stack of six sheets. Lift them up and fit into the buttered dish, covering the base and sides. Press them gently into the corners of the dish to make a nest for the filling. Pour the filling on top and smooth the surface.

Make another stack of six buttered filo sheets. Lift this onto the pie, covering the filling. Press the two overhanging layers of filo together, trimming these to a couple of centimetres (about an inch).

**continues on next page …**

**120 g (4¼ oz) unsalted butter,**
    **melted to golden**
**12 sheets filo pastry, at least**
    **38 x 30 cm (15 x 12 inches) in size**

**SYRUP**
**280 g (10 oz) sugar**
**1 long strip of lemon peel**

**FILLING**
**225 g (8 oz) sugar**
**75 g (2½ oz) fine semolina**
**20 g (¾ oz) cornflour (cornstarch)**
**4 egg yolks, plus 2 whole eggs**
**1.5 litres (52 fl oz/6 cups) milk**
**2 teaspoons vanilla extract**
**a nice grating of fresh nutmeg**

Roll these edges over on themselves to seal the filling in. Using a sharp knife, gently score the top pastry into 12 pieces, only cutting through the top sheet or two of filo. Flick a little cold water here and there (to prevent the filo curling). Bake until crisp and golden, about 25 minutes. Remove from the oven, rest for a couple of minutes then pour the syrup over the top, covering all the pie. Now leave for at least 1 hour before serving to allow the syrup to settle as the pie cools.

This will keep for a number of days if left, covered with a tea towel, in a cool dry place (not refrigerated).

The filo sheets need to be large enough to cover the base and sides of a 30 x 22 cm (12 x 8½ inch) dish. If yours are smaller, use more sheets and cut to fit.

# FILO MILLEFEUILLE WITH ORANGES

This always reminds me of Athens and the avenues lined with orange trees. I have also made this with pomegranates, juicing one or two and following the same method for the orange sauce here. Or use both and scatter pomegranate seeds and orange slices around the plate: the colours look beautiful together.

Slice the tops and bottoms off the oranges. To fillet the oranges, sit them on a board. With a small sharp knife, cut downwards to remove the skin and pith. Hold the orange over a bowl and remove the fillets by slicing in between the white pith. Remove the pips. You should be left with an orange 'skeleton'. Put the fillets in the bowl and squeeze out the remaining juice from the skeletons, then discard the skeletons.

To make the orange confit, put the ingredients in a small saucepan and simmer for 7–8 minutes, until a jam forms.

To make the sauce, put all the ingredients in a saucepan and pour in the juice from the orange fillets as well. Boil until thickened and reduced.

To make the sabayon cream, put the gelatine in a small bowl (you can snap the leaf if necessary), cover with cold water and leave it to soften completely. Put the whole egg, egg yolks and sugar in a heatproof bowl over a saucepan of simmering water, making sure the bottom of the bowl isn't touching the water. Whisk constantly for about 12–15 minutes or until the mixture is thick and fluffy.

continues on next page …

**SERVES 8**

5 oranges
3 sheets filo pastry
60 g (2¼ oz) butter, melted
30 g (1 oz) sugar
3 tablespoons runny honey

**ORANGE CONFIT**
grated zest and juice of 1 orange
30 g (1 oz) sugar

**ORANGE SAUCE**
juice of 3 oranges
15 g (½ oz) butter
30 g (1 oz) sugar
1 tablespoon Grand Marnier, port or
   Vin Santo

**SABAYON CREAM**
1 x 2 g gelatine leaf
1 egg, plus 2 egg yolks
50 g (1¾ oz) sugar
1 teaspoon orange blossom water
300 ml (10½ fl oz) whipping cream

icing (confectioners') sugar, to serve

Whisk in 2 teaspoons of the confit and the orange blossom water and take the bowl off the saucepan. (If there's any confit left you can add it to the cream or oranges at the last minute, or serve it over ice cream.)

Squeeze out all the water from the gelatine with your hands and whisk the gelatine into the sabayon cream, making sure it is well incorporated. Now whip the cream to soft peaks and fold this into the sabayon. Leave in a cool place, even in the fridge, until you are ready to use it.

Preheat the oven to 180°C (350°F/Gas 4). Place a sheet of filo pastry on a work surface, brush with melted butter and sprinkle the surface evenly with half the sugar. Place another sheet of filo on the first, brush with butter and sprinkle with the remaining sugar. Add the last sheet of filo, brushing with butter. Cut the filo in half horizontally and then cut each half into 12 strips, giving you a total of 24 rectangles. Put them on a baking tray lined with baking paper, drizzle the honey in long thin lines all over the filo and bake for 10 minutes, or until crisp and golden brown. Set aside to cool on a clean sheet of baking paper so that they don't stick.

To serve, place a filo rectangle on each plate. Add a good dollop of sabayon cream, a few orange segments, another layer of filo, more sabayon and orange segments and a final layer of filo. Scatter a few orange segments around the plate, drizzle with sauce, dust the top with icing sugar and serve.

# BAKED CINNAMON APPLES WITH BUTTERMILK ICE CREAM

This is the sort of thing I like to eat on Christmas Eve — quite healthy and homely and just delicious. We eat it with teaspoons, scraping the soft apple out of the skins and eating it with the juice and ice cream. You'll need an ovenproof dish that's about 26 x 20 cm (10½ x 8 inches) and just large enough to take the eight apple halves compactly. You could bake the apples in advance, cover them with foil and then just heat them up a bit before serving.

For the ice cream, whisk the cream with the sugar and vanilla until all the sugar has dissolved and the cream starts to thicken. Add the buttermilk, whisking it in to incorporate and then pour into a bowl or container that has a lid. Put the lid on and put in the freezer. After an hour give the mixture an energetic whisk with a hand whisk or electric mixer. Put it back in the freezer and then whisk again after another couple of hours. When the ice cream is nearly firm, give one last whisk and put it back in the freezer to set. Alternatively, pour it into your ice-cream machine and churn, following the manufacturer's instructions.

Preheat the oven to 180°C (350°F/Gas 4) and use some of the butter to grease a shallow ovenproof dish, just large enough to fit all 8 apple halves quite compactly. Halve the apples and neatly core them, making sure you don't pierce the skin. Arrange them in the baking dish, cut side up. Mix the sugar and cinnamon and sprinkle over the apples. Put a blob of butter on each apple, sprinkle the Marsala over the top and dribble 125 ml (4 fl oz/ ½ cup) of water around the dish.

Bake for about 30 minutes, then dribble the pan juices over the apples and add another 125 ml (4 fl oz/½ cup) of hot water to the dish. Bake for another 30 minutes or so, or until the apples are soft inside and golden on top but still have their shape. Serve warm or at room temperature, with some sauce spooned over the apples and a scoop or two of the ice cream.

SERVES 4 (ALTHOUGH THERE WILL BE ICE CREAM LEFT OVER FOR ANOTHER TIME)

**BUTTERMILK ICE CREAM**
250 ml (9 fl oz/1 cup) thin (pouring) cream
200 g (7 oz) caster (superfine) sugar
1 teaspoon vanilla extract
500 ml (17 fl oz/2 cups) buttermilk

50 g (1¾ oz) butter
4 lovely apples, cored and halved
80 g (2¾ oz) light brown sugar
1 teaspoon ground cinnamon
2 tablespoons Marsala or port

# CHOCOLATE CAKE WITH ICING

This is exactly the kind of chocolate cake I loved as a child. Sometimes I make this just chocolate, sometimes halved and filled with not-too-sweet raspberry or strawberry jam or purée and a few dollops of cream (and then I don't ice it). If you like, you might also add some chopped nuts in with the flour or scatter some over the top.

Preheat the oven to 180°C (350°F/Gas 4). Butter and flour a 24 cm (9½ inch) springform cake tin. Melt the butter in a small saucepan over low heat, then add the chocolate and cocoa and stir until melted. Remove from the heat. Whisk the egg whites in a bowl until they are creamy and stiff. In another bowl, whisk the egg yolks until they are foamy, then beat in the sugar. Add the chocolate mixture, a bit at a time initially to acclimatise the eggs. Next, sift in the flour and baking powder and mix well. Add the milk and mix until smooth.

Carefully fold in the beaten whites, trying not to deflate them, and gently mix until they are completely incorporated into a fluffy but dense mixture. Scrape out into the tin and bake for about 30–35 minutes. Remove from the oven and cool completely in the tin before moving to a serving plate.

For the icing, whip the butter with the icing sugar until fluffy. Whisk in the cocoa a bit at a time so that it doesn't fly everywhere. When it is completely incorporated, add the milk and golden syrup and whisk until very smooth. Spread it over the top of the cake with a spatula, using swift smooth strokes. I like it not completely smooth but in chocolate waves.

**CUTS INTO 10–12 SLICES**

180 g (6½ oz) butter

50 g (1¾ oz) dark (semi-sweet) chocolate, broken up

30 g (1 oz/¼ cup) unsweetened cocoa powder

3 eggs, separated

180 g (6½ oz) caster (superfine) sugar

125 g (4½ oz) plain (all-purpose) flour

1½ teaspoons baking powder

3 tablespoons milk

**ICING**

80 g (2¾ oz) butter, softened

60 g (2¼ oz/½ cup) icing (confectioners') sugar

30 g (1 oz/¼ cup) unsweetened cocoa powder

2 tablespoons milk

2 generous teaspoons golden syrup

# BERRY CHEESECAKE

If you are using frozen berries, leave them in a bowl to come to room temperature before you start (you probably won't need to add any water when you sauté them later). Raspberries on their own are beautiful here, but choose your favourite berries or use a mixture. Blueberries, blackberries and strawberries all work well. You can leave out the cornflour when you heat the berries, if you prefer, but the berries won't hold onto the cake so well. Or simply serve a slice of plain cheesecake with a spoonful of berries on the side.

SERVES 8

Preheat your oven to 180°C (350°F/Gas 4). Grease a 24 cm (9½ inch) springform cake tin. Mix together the crushed biscuits and melted butter. Press the biscuit mix into the tin so that it covers the base and comes about two-thirds of the way up the side, kneading down with your palms to push it along evenly.

Whisk the cream cheese in a bowl with 200 g (7 oz) of the sugar. Beat in the eggs one by one and then the vanilla until you have a smooth thick cream. Pour over the base and smooth the top with a spatula. Bake for about 40–50 minutes, until it is lightly golden in parts and wobbles only a little when you shake the tin. Cool completely, then chill in the fridge for a few hours.

Meanwhile, mix the cornflour with a couple of tablespoons of cold water until it is smooth. Pour into a saucepan to heat up, then add the berries, grated lemon zest and the remaining sugar — the amount of sugar may depend on the sweetness of the berries. Cook for a couple of minutes, adding some water if it seems too thick, to just combine everything and then remove from the heat before the berries collapse. Set aside to cool completely.

Carefully remove the ring from the cheesecake and spoon the berries over the top. Cut into wedges to serve. If you are not serving it immediately, keep the cake in the fridge.

250 g (9 oz) digestive biscuits, coarsely crushed in a blender

125 g (4½ oz) unsalted butter, melted, plus a little extra

750 g (1 lb 10 oz) cream cheese

250 g (9 oz) caster (superfine) sugar

4 eggs

1 teaspoon vanilla extract

2 teaspoons cornflour (cornstarch)

400 g (14 oz) fresh or frozen berries

1 teaspoon finely grated lemon zest

# JAM & CREAM SHORTCAKE

This is another cake that my mother makes often. It is delicious, honest and quick and easy to make. It doesn't keep very well once it is filled so, if you won't be serving it immediately, keep the cake covered in plastic wrap once it has cooled and just cut it and spread with the jam and cream before serving. Use any flavour jam you like — just not too sweet. I love this with homemade quince and grape jam. If you don't have any jam, you could use fresh berries.

Preheat the oven to 190°C (375°F/Gas 5). Grease and flour a 24 cm (9½ inch) springform cake tin.

Sift the flour into a bowl with the sugar, baking powder and a pinch of salt. Add the butter and use an electric mixer or wooden spoon to quickly mix it together. Whisk the egg and milk together in a small bowl and add to the batter. Mix in quickly to incorporate it. You should have a soft thick batter.

Pour the batter into the cake tin and bake for about 30 minutes, or until the cake is lightly golden. Remove from the oven and cool slightly, then remove from the cake tin and leave to cool completely.

Slice the cake in half horizontally. Slide the bottom half onto a serving plate. Whisk the vanilla into the cream so that it is quite stiff. Spread the jam over the bottom layer of cake and then carefully spread the cream over the jam. Cover with the top layer of the cake and dust with icing sugar.

**SERVES 8**

250 g (9 oz) cake flour or plain (all-purpose) flour, plus extra for dusting

120 g (4¼ oz) sugar

2 teaspoons baking powder

120 g (4¼ oz) butter, softened, plus extra for greasing

1 egg

185 ml (6 fl oz/¾ cup) milk

1 teaspoon vanilla extract

300 ml (10½ fl oz) thick (double) cream

200 g (7 oz) homemade jam (not too sweet)

icing (confectioners') sugar, to serve

# HONEY CAKE

I hope you are lucky enough to have tiny purple flowers on your
rosemary when you make this, so you can scatter them over the
finished cake.

Grease and line the base of a 22 cm (8½ inch) springform cake tin. Put the
butter, brown sugar and honey in a small saucepan and add 1 tablespoon of
water. Heat gently, stirring once or twice, until the butter melts and the sugar
dissolves. Leave to cool for 15 minutes. Preheat the oven to 180°C (350°F/
Gas 4).

Sift the flour, baking powder and cinnamon into a bowl and add the
rosemary. Add the honey mixture and eggs and beat until smooth.

Pour into the tin and bake for 35–40 minutes, or until a skewer comes out
clean when you poke it into the centre. Leave in the tin to cool completely.

To make the lemon icing, sift the icing sugar into a bowl. Add the butter,
lemon zest and juice and 1 tablespoon of water and beat until smooth. You
might like to add a few more drops of lemon juice after tasting it. Spread over
the top and side of the cake. The cake softens as it sits and will keep well for
up to a week in a cake tin.

**CUTS INTO 8–10 SLICES**

150 g (5½ oz) butter
115 g (4 oz) dark brown sugar
175 g (6 oz/½ cup) honey
200 g (7 oz) plain (all-purpose) flour
1½ teaspoons baking powder
½ teaspoon ground cinnamon
1 tablespoon finely chopped
    rosemary leaves
2 eggs, beaten

**LEMON ICING**
250 g (9 oz/2 cups) icing
    (confectioners') sugar
100 g (3½ oz) butter, softened
1 teaspoon grated lemon zest
2 tablespoons lemon juice

# CARROT CAKE

This is one of those classic cakes that can disappear for a year or two, but I would always welcome back a slice from time to time with an afternoon coffee, or even for breakfast. This recipe is my friend Annette's. Every time she makes it people ask her for the recipe ... so I did too.

**SERVES ABOUT 10**

Preheat your oven to 180°C (350°F/Gas 4). Grease and flour a 24 cm (9½ inch) fluted ring (bundt) tin or springform cake tin.

Whip together the eggs and sugar until creamy, then whisk in the oil. Sift together the flour, salt, baking powder, bicarbonate of soda and cinnamon. Add to the egg mixture and whisk to combine. Add the carrot and walnuts and mix through quickly with an electric mixer to make sure it is all properly combined. Scrape out the batter into the tin. Bake for about an hour, or until a skewer inserted into the centre comes out clean. The cake should have risen up impressively high. Cool a little before turning out onto a plate.

While the cake is baking, make the icing. Whip together the butter and icing sugar, mashing it together at first with a wooden spoon and then whisking until it is stiff. Quickly beat in the cream cheese and vanilla to just combine.

When the cake is cool, spread the icing over the top and side with a spatula (you don't need to spread it too smoothly, it looks better in peaks).

4 eggs, lightly beaten

250 g (9 oz) caster (superfine) sugar

185 ml (6 fl oz/¾ cup) sunflower or light olive oil

300 g (10½ oz) cake flour or plain (all-purpose) flour

¾ teaspoon salt

2 teaspoons baking powder

1 teaspoon bicarbonate of soda (baking soda)

2 teaspoons ground cinnamon

400 g (14 oz) carrots, peeled and grated

55 g (2 oz/½ cup) chopped walnuts

**ICING**

180 g (6½ oz) butter, softened

250 g (9 oz/2 cups) icing (confectioners') sugar

180 g (6½ oz) cream cheese

3 drops vanilla extract

# CHOCOLATE TRUFFLE TART WITH HOT CHOCOLATE

Serve this in small portions: it is enough for eight people and is just on the right side of richness in a tiny slice. On its own it is gorgeous with a pile of fresh fruit and another pile of crème fraîche. If you prefer an icing to the little espresso cups of wintry hot chocolate, then melt 150 ml (5 fl oz) of cream with 150 g (5½ oz) of chocolate and pour over the cooled cake.

Preheat the oven to 180°C (350°F/Gas 4). Butter and flour a 20 cm (8 inch) springform cake tin. Melt the butter in a small saucepan over low heat. Add the sugar and chocolate and stir until the chocolate melts and the sugar dissolves. Remove from the heat and scrape into a mixing bowl. Leave to cool for about 30 minutes. Add the egg yolks and vanilla and whisk in well with an electric mixer. Sift in the flour and whisk until well combined, then fold in the hazelnuts.

Whip the egg whites until very fluffy and then fold through the chocolate mixture a spoonful at a time. Scrape the mixture into the cake tin and bake for about 35 minutes, or until a skewer inserted comes out clean and the cake feels firm and is a little cracked on the top. Leave to cool for at least 15 minutes or so before you remove it from the tin.

To make the hot chocolate, put the cream in a saucepan and bring to the boil. Add the chocolate, stirring until it is thick and smooth and the chocolate has completely melted. Pour into espresso cups and serve with little wedges of cake.

**SERVES 8**

100 g (3½ oz) butter, plus extra for greasing

100 g (3½ oz) caster (superfine) sugar

100 g (3½ oz) dark semi-sweet chocolate, broken into pieces

3 eggs, separated

1 teaspoon vanilla extract

20 g (¾ oz) cake flour or plain (all-purpose) flour, plus extra for dusting

40 g (1½ oz) finely ground hazelnuts

**HOT CHOCOLATE**

375 ml (13 fl oz/1½ cups) thin (pouring) cream

100 g (3½ oz) dark semi-sweet chocolate, broken into pieces

# RICOTTA TART WITH A CHOCOLATE CRUST

This is a typical southern Italy combination of flavours: ricotta, the burstingly ripe oranges and, every Italian's obsession, chocolate. It is quite simple to make, so don't be intimidated by the thought of the pastry crust. If it seems too soft, just add more flour as you're rolling it, then lift it over your rolling pin and gently lower it into the tin. If it breaks, just patchwork it in.

To make the pastry base, use a food processor to mix together the butter and sugar until pale and creamy. Sift in the flour and cocoa and then beat in the egg to make a nice soft pastry. Scrape out onto plastic wrap, flatten into a disc and wrap up. Refrigerate for about an hour.

Preheat your oven to 180°C (350°F/Gas 4). Roll out the pastry on a lightly floured work surface until large enough to line a 24 cm (9½ inch) loose-bottomed tart tin or springform cake tin with high sides. Line the pastry with baking paper and baking beans or uncooked rice and bake for about 20 minutes. Remove the paper and beans and bake for a further 5 minutes to slightly dry the base.

For the filling, whisk together the eggs and sugar until thick and creamy. Whisk in the orange zest and ricotta until smooth. Whisk in the lemon and orange juice then scrape the filling into your pastry case. Bake for about 30–40 minutes, or until the top seems set and is lightly golden here and there. Cool before cutting into portions. This can be served slightly warm, at room temperature or even cold from the fridge.

SERVES 8–10

100 g (3½ oz) butter, slightly softened

85 g (3 oz) caster (superfine) sugar

150 g (5½ oz) plain (all-purpose) flour

30 g (1 oz/¼ cup) unsweetened cocoa powder

1 egg, beaten

**FILLING**

3 eggs, beaten

140 g (5 oz) caster (superfine) sugar

1 heaped teaspoon finely grated orange zest

750 g (1 lb 10 oz) smooth ricotta cheese

1 tablespoon lemon juice

2 tablespoons orange juice

# MILK TART

Milk tart was something we ate often in South Africa; it was on the menu in many tea rooms and bakeries. You might like to make double the pastry and freeze it ready rolled-out in the tin so that you can whip it straight into the oven whenever you need to produce a pudding in a rush.

To make the pastry, mix the butter and sugar together with a wooden spoon until softened. Add the flour, baking powder and a pinch of salt and mix with your fingers until damp and sandy. Add the egg and knead very gently so that the pastry comes together. Flatten a little and wrap in plastic. Refrigerate for 1 hour before rolling out. Preheat your oven to 180°C (350°F/Gas 4).

Roll out the pastry on a floured work surface to line a 26 cm (10½ inch) tart tin with sides at least 3 cm (1¼ inches) high. Line with baking paper, fill with baking beans or uncooked rice and blind bake for 20 minutes. Remove the beans and paper when the visible pastry is golden. Prick the pastry base a few times with a fork and bake for a further 10 minutes to dry out the bottom.

Meanwhile, make the filling. Put the milk and butter in a pan over medium heat to melt the butter. Whisk the egg yolks with the sugar and vanilla, then whisk in the cornflour. Add a ladleful of the hot milk to the eggs, whisking to avoid scrambling them. Add the rest of the milk, mix it all together well and leave to cool. Whisk the egg whites to soft peaks, then gradually fold into the filling. Pour into the tart case, sprinkle the sugar and cinnamon over the top and return to the oven for 30 minutes, or until it is set and just a bit wobbly. Cool before serving.

**SERVES 8**

**PASTRY**
100 g (3½ oz) cold butter, cut into cubes
100 g (3½ oz) caster (superfine) sugar
230 g (8 oz) cake flour or plain (all-purpose) flour
½ teaspoon baking powder
1 egg, lightly beaten

**FILLING**
750 ml (26 fl oz/3 cups) milk
75 g (2½ oz) butter
3 eggs, separated
100 g (3½ oz) caster (superfine) sugar
1 teaspoon vanilla extract
30 g (1 oz/¼ cup) cornflour (cornstarch)

1 tablespoon sugar
1 teaspoon ground cinnamon

# PEPPERMINT CRISP PIE

This outrageous pie is a base of crushed biscuits, a layer of caramel, a layer of whipped cream and then a scattering of crisp peppermint milk chocolate. It is incredibly rich and should probably be served in small spoonfuls, depending, of course, on your personal tastes. It makes me think of boarding school midnight feasts in books from the 1950s. You need to use chocolate bars with an apple-green crunchy filling, not a soft creamy centre. In South Africa we made this with 'tennis' biscuits, but digestives work just as well. It is possible to buy the condensed milk already boiled into caramel. If you can't get it, you will have to simmer the tins in a large pot of water for about 3½ hours so the condensed milk turns nutty golden brown. Let the tins cool in the pot before removing and opening them — your condensed milk should be caramelised.

SERVES 10–12

Crush the biscuits and put them in a bowl with the butter. Mix together well and then press firmly onto the base and a little way up the sides of a 26 cm (10½ inch) pie dish. Put in the fridge to set.

Beat the caramel in a bowl with a wooden spoon until smooth. Carefully spread over the biscuit base, trying not to lift any of the biscuit crumbs.

Whip the cream until it holds its shape well, but take care not to overwhip it. Spoon it over the caramel to cover the whole surface and then scatter the peppermint chocolate over the top. Keep in the fridge before serving in slices if you can manage it, or dollops if you can't. This is also good the next day.

250 g (9 oz) digestive biscuits (graham crackers)

100 g (3½ oz) butter, melted

600 g (1 lb 5 oz/1½ tins) caramel condensed milk

400 ml (14 fl oz) whipping cream

100 g (3½ oz) peppermint crisp bars, crumbled or coarsely grated

# PINEAPPLE CAKE

This is a very popular cake in Portugal and is lovely for breakfast, afternoon tea or as an anytime snack. I had this very often while I was there, made with their lovely pineapples. If you can't get a fresh pineapple then tinned will do, and this is also beautiful made with apple slices. You can also bake it in a high ring (bundt) tin if that's what you have in your cupboard. In Portugal it's very often made that way.

CUTS INTO ABOUT 12 SLICES

350 g (12 oz) caster (superfine) sugar

1 fresh pineapple (about 650 g/ 1 lb 7 oz)

4 eggs, separated

200 g (7 oz) unsalted butter

200 g (7 oz) cake flour or plain (all-purpose) flour

1 teaspoon baking powder

Heat your oven to 180°C (350°F/Gas 4) and grease a 30 x 11 cm (12 x 4 inch) loaf (bar) tin. Flour the tin very lightly, then rap on your work surface to remove any excess. To make the caramel, tip 115 g (4 oz) of the caster sugar into a heavy-based non-stick pan over medium heat and add a couple of teaspoons of water. Heat it up until the sugar starts to melt, then tilt the pan to swirl it around — don't stir or the sugar will crystallise. Carry on heating and swirling a few times until all the sugar has melted and turned golden caramel brown; watch carefully, it can burn in a few seconds. Pour carefully into the tin, tilting so the caramel covers the bottom. Leave to cool.

Peel your pineapple and cut out any eyes. Cut into 1 cm (½ inch) rings, then twizzle out the core and eat or discard it. You will need about ten nice rings. Arrange the rings over the base of the tin, overlapping them as much as possible. (Try to imagine how it will look when you turn it upside down to serve.)

Whip the egg whites into soft peaks. Cream together the butter and the remaining sugar. Add the egg yolks, beating them in well, then sift in the flour and baking powder. Fold in the egg whites.

Spoon into the tin, over and around the pineapple, tapping the tin on the work surface to settle it in.

Bake for about 55–60 minutes, until the top is puffed and beautifully golden and a skewer comes out fairly clean when poked into the middle (this will still be quite a moist cake). Cool for a while, then loosen the sides with a knife and turn out. Cut into thick slices to serve, either warm or completely cooled.

# PECAN BUTTER BISCUITS

Made without the icing, these biscuits are gorgeous with the maple syrup ice cream on the following page. Although I love the pecans here, you might like to try it with another nut — perhaps walnuts or hazelnuts. This will give you about 40 biscuits. You might like to ice yours with a soft creamy icing tinted with your favourite colour.

Preheat your oven to 190°C (375°F/Gas 5). Cream the butter with the icing sugar and vanilla until it is smooth. Add the flour in four portions, mashing it in well with a wooden spoon after each addition. Mix the nuts through.

Divide the dough into quarters. Dip your fingers in icing sugar and then, from each quarter of dough, roll 10 balls the size of cherry tomatoes. Put on two ungreased baking trays, leaving some space between each ball. Flatten each one a bit, and then dip your thumb in icing sugar and make an indent in each ball. The icing sugar will sit in there and, even if you're not icing the biscuits, it'll look good.

Bake one tray at a time for about 15 minutes or until the biscuits are firm and golden, and slightly darker around the edges. Bake for a few more minutes, if necessary. They are delicate, so carefully lift them off the trays and onto racks to cool. Wait until they are completely cold if you are going to ice them, otherwise store them in a biscuit tin.

To make the icing, cream together the icing sugar, butter, vanilla and milk until completely smooth. You may need to use more or less milk to get a soft, buttery consistency. Add the food colouring, mixing it in well. If you are not ready to ice the biscuits immediately, cover the bowl with a wet paper towel.

Use a small butter knife or a teaspoon to spread the icing quite rustically into and over the indentations in the biscuits. When the icing has hardened a little, store the biscuits in a tin. They keep very well at room temperature.

**MAKES 40**

220 g (7¾ oz) butter, softened

70 g (2½ oz) icing (confectioners') sugar, plus a little extra for dusting

1 teaspoon vanilla extract

280 g (10 oz) plain (all-purpose) flour

70 g (2½ oz) pecans, chopped

**ICING**

250 g (9 oz) icing (confectioners') sugar

30 g (1 oz) butter, softened

1 teaspoon vanilla extract

2 tablespoons milk

a few drops of food colouring

# MAPLE SYRUP & VANILLA ICE CREAM

I am crazy about this with the pecan butter biscuits on the previous page. You could also sauté some chopped walnuts or pecans in butter and then fold them through when the ice cream is just about ready. This will keep for up to a week in the freezer.

**SERVES 6–8**

Mix together the cream and maple syrup in a bowl or container that has a lid. Whisk in the milk and vanilla. Put the lid on the bowl and put it in the freezer. After an hour give the mixture an energetic whisk with a hand whisk or electric mixer. Put it back in the freezer and then whisk again after another couple of hours. When the ice cream is nearly firm, give one last whisk and put it back in the freezer to set.

Alternatively, pour it into your ice-cream machine and churn, following the manufacturer's instructions.

250 ml (9 fl oz/1 cup) thin (pouring) cream

125 ml (4 fl oz/½ cup) pure maple syrup

250 ml (9 fl oz/1 cup) milk

1 teaspoon vanilla extract

# CRUMBLER CAKE

Be prepared to tread on crumbs around the table after eating *sbriciolona*. *Sbriciolare* is Italian for 'crumble', and that's exactly what the name implies: crumbly. This is beautiful with sweetened whipped or thick cream that the crumbs can cling to, or just with a glass of something moscato-ish. In Venice, fragolino, a red or white sweet wine, is what they like to drink.

SERVES 8–10

Preheat your oven to 180°C (350°F/Gas 4). Use a blob from the butter to grease a 28 cm (11¼ inch) springform cake tin and lightly dust it with flour. Put the almonds in a food processor and pulse until quite fine but with some chunks left (alternatively, bash them with your rolling pin).

Whip the egg with the sugar and vanilla until nice and creamy. Put the softened butter on a plate and mash until smooth but not melted. Gradually whisk the flour, butter and a pinch of salt into the egg mixture. Add the ground almonds and work them in with your hands to make a rough pastry.

Pat the mixture into your tin, dollops at a time, flattening it to roughly cover the base. It won't look perfect but will spread while baking. Bake for about 40 minutes until golden brown.

Cool, then cut into wedges if you can (it's crumbly). To serve, either whip some cream with a little vanilla extract and sugar, or simply serve with thick cream that holds the crumbs in its cloud of thickness.

200 g (9 oz) unpeeled almonds
1 egg
140 g (5 oz/⅔ cup) sugar
1 teaspoon vanilla extract
250 g (9 oz) unsalted butter, softened
250 g (9 oz) plain (all-purpose) flour
whipped cream or ice cream, to serve

# POACHED FRUIT IN VANILLA SYRUP

This is just fruit served in a bath of syrup. Use any fruit you like but I feel colour is important here, so a couple of berries or cherries can be splashed in at the last moment if you don't have very red plums. Choose fruit with a beautiful shape. I love serving something like this with a scoop of snow-white yoghurt or buttermilk ice cream (see page 297). This is lovely for breakfast or dessert or just as a snack. Ladle any leftover syrup into cups for children to drink. You could also add different spices to your poaching syrup — a small cinnamon stick, cloves, a bay leaf, for instance.

**SERVES 5–6**

2 small ripe but firm pears

3 bright-red ripe, but firm, plums

2 juicy, but firm, peaches or nectarines

a handful of seedless green and black grapes

200 g (7 oz) caster (superfine) sugar

1 strip lemon or lime peel, pith removed

juice of ½ a lemon or lime

½ a vanilla bean, split in half lengthways

Peel the pears, keeping their smooth shape. Halve lengthways and cut out the cores. Halve the unpeeled plums lengthways and remove their stones by gently twisting the halves. If the stones are stubborn, edge them out with a spoon or the point of a potato peeler. Cut each half in half again lengthways, if they are large. Do the same with the peaches or nectarines and halve the grapes too.

Put 1 litre (35 fl oz/4 cups) of cold water in a large saucepan and add the sugar, lemon or lime peel and the juice. Scrape the seeds from the vanilla bean into the pan and then throw in the bean as well. Bring to the boil and then simmer for about 5 minutes. Lower the heat and add the fruit you think will take the longest (probably the pears). Poach them gently for about 5 minutes, turning them with a slotted spoon so that they are totally immersed in syrup and don't darken in parts. Add the plums and peaches and carry on simmering for another 5 minutes or so, just until they surrender their firmness and have absorbed the syrup (not too long, or they will become soggy). Next add the grapes, which will only need a couple of minutes. In the meantime, if some of the fruit looks ready, remove it very carefully with the slotted spoon and put in a wide bowl, taking care not to mark the fruits with cuts or dents. If you have overdone it at any stage, pop the bowl into the freezer for a few minutes to cool the fruit down and stop it cooking further.

Cool the fruits at room temperature in a fly-free zone. If the skins of the peaches are wrinkled, slip them off. Otherwise leave them on, and leave the plum skins on, too. When the syrup has cooled, pour it over the fruit. Serve very slightly warm or at room temperature, and it is even good cold from the fridge in summer. This will keep well in the fridge, covered, for up to five days.

# POMEGRANATE SORBET

I make this when I have lovely rosy pomegranates. The colour of your sorbet will vary in intensity, depending on the colour of your pomegranate seeds. Sometimes I serve this on its own and sometimes with a scoop of vanilla ice cream.

SERVES 4

4 ripe pomegranates
juice of 1 lemon
120 g (4¼ oz) caster (superfine) sugar

Juice the pomegranates very thoroughly, using a levered juice extractor or a citrus juicer, and then strain. You should have about 435 ml (15¼ fl oz/ 1¾ cups) of juice. Put the lemon juice in a small saucepan with the sugar and 2–3 tablespoons of the pomegranate juice. Heat, stirring, over medium–low heat until the sugar has dissolved. Remove from the heat, leave to cool a little and then stir in the rest of the pomegranate juice.

Pour the mixture into a bowl or container that has a lid. Put the lid on and put it in the freezer. After an hour give the mixture an energetic whisk with a hand whisk or electric mixer. Put it back in the freezer and then whisk again after another couple of hours. When the sorbet is nearly firm, give one last whisk and put it back in the freezer to set. Alternatively, pour it into your ice-cream machine and churn, following the manufacturer's instructions.

# BUTTER SUGAR BISCUITS

These really do melt in your mouth. The Greeks call these *kourapiedes*, and you can serve them on their own with tea, coffee, a liqueur or just a glass of iced water. You will find you really have to eat these over a plate or pop a whole one in your mouth at once so that the icing sugar doesn't fly everywhere. You will use a lot of icing sugar for dusting: you can always recycle some from the bottom, or sieve the leftover sugar of crumbs and put it back in your tin.

Preheat the oven to 180°C (350°F/Gas 4) and line a baking tray with a sheet of baking paper.

Using electric beaters, beat the butter for 8–10 minutes until it is very pale and thick. Add the 2 tablespoons of icing sugar, beating it in well. Add the egg yolk and vanilla and whisk until well incorporated, then mix in the brandy. Sift in the flour and baking powder, mixing until you have a thick dough that becomes difficult to mix with the electric mixer. Scoop up softly in your hands, cover in plastic wrap and refrigerate for about 30 minutes.

Form the dough into small balls about the size of cherry tomatoes (these are often made into crescent shapes too) and put them on the tray, leaving a little space between them.

Bake for about 20 minutes or until they are lightly golden. Remove from the oven and leave to cool for 10–15 minutes. Meanwhile, line another tray with baking paper and sprinkle with half of the extra icing sugar. Take the slightly cooled biscuits and place them in one layer on top of the icing sugar. Sprinkle the rest of the icing sugar over the top (the biscuits should be almost buried in the sugar). Keep these in an airtight container.

**MAKES 45**

250 g (9 oz) butter

2 tablespoons icing (confectioners') sugar, plus about 300 g (10½ oz) for dusting

1 egg yolk

1 teaspoon vanilla extract

1 tablespoon brandy

300 g (10½ oz) cake flour or plain (all-purpose) flour, sifted

1 teaspoon baking powder

# MERINGUE WITH STRAWBERRIES & CHOCOLATE

This is my friend Sue's meringue. It's well dressed, showy — quite over-the-top — and easy to make. You can add a little icing sugar to your cream as you whip it, if you like your sweet things very sweet. I whip it without and just shake a little sugar over the top of the cake to serve. This is lovely with strawberries, blackberries or raspberries, served in rough slices with a big cup of milky tea.

Preheat the oven to 120°C (235°F/Gas ½). Cover the base of a 24 cm (9½ inch) springform cake tin with a sheet of baking paper before clipping the side in place. The paper will stick out of the side, making it easier to remove the meringue later. Grease the side of the tin.

Whisk the egg whites in a bowl until they lose their foaminess and look like very thick, stiff shaving cream. Whisk in the sugar bit by bit until it is all incorporated, then whisk in the vanilla and the vinegar. Gently but thoroughly fold in the nuts and crackers. Spoon into the tin and level the surface, making a slight indent in the middle.

Bake for about 1¼–1½ hours, until the meringue is lightly golden and coming away from the side of the tin. Turn off the oven, prop the door just slightly ajar and leave the meringue inside until it is completely cool. Take the meringue out of the tin and put it on a serving plate, removing the baking paper.

Melt the dark chocolate in the top of a double boiler, making sure that the water doesn't touch the bottom of the bowl. Drizzle over the meringue in a criss-cross pattern and then leave to harden completely.

Whip the cream with the vanilla until it holds thickly on the beaters. Dollop onto the meringue, leaving a small border to show off the chocolate. Dot the berries on top and cover with a gentle shake of icing sugar to serve.

SERVES 8

**MERINGUE**

4 egg whites

160 g (5½ oz) caster (superfine) sugar

1 teaspoon vanilla extract

2 teaspoons apple cider vinegar

60 g (2¼ oz/½ cup) finely chopped walnuts or hazelnuts

60 g (2¼ oz) unsalted crackers, finely crushed

**TOPPING**

140 g (5 oz) dark (semi-sweet) chocolate

250 ml (9 fl oz/1 cup) whipping cream

1 teaspoon vanilla extract

150 g (5½ oz) strawberries, hulled

icing (confectioners') sugar, to serve

# ROSE CAKE

This recipe is from Marzia, one of my neighbours in Italy, who got it from someone in Venice, but it is traditionally a Portuguese cake. (It must have fallen off one of the old ships travelling the spice route from Portugal to Venice!) It's often made with some chopped-up candied fruits and other bits and pieces folded in.

Crumble up the fresh yeast (or sprinkle the dried) into a small bowl, add the lukewarm milk and a stolen pinch of the sugar and whisk it together. Leave until the yeast starts to activate and bubble up a bit. Add about a cupful of flour, or however much it takes to make a soft dough. Knead briefly into a smooth ball, make a cross on top and put it in a large bowl. Cover with a cloth and leave to rise in a warm place for 1½–2 hours until doubled in size or well puffed up.

Whip together the egg, yolks and cream and then add to the risen dough with the 115 g of sugar and the rest of the flour, saving a few spoonfuls for kneading and rolling. Mix well with your fingers to separate any clumps and make it all into a soft smooth dough. Use a heavy-duty mixer for this, if you have one.

Knead the pastry on the largest board you have or just on your work surface (the diameter of this pastry will be 70 cm/27½ inches!). Roll out into a circle, dusting your hands with flour to prevent sticking, until about 2 mm (¹⁄₁₆ inch) thick and 70 cm (27½ inches) across. Butter a 30 cm (12 inch) round non-stick cake tin that is about 6 cm (2½ inches) deep. Mash up the butter with the extra sugar until soft, creamy and easy to spread. Dab it here and there over the pastry and then gently spread with a butter knife or your hands. Roll up fairly tightly into a long thin sausage.

Cut into 5 cm (2 inch) sections (I got about 15 or 16 roses from my pastry). Stand them upright on your work surface and make about 5 shallow snips around the edge with kitchen scissors. Arrange, standing up, in the tin — one in the middle, some around the outside and a few smaller ones in the middle row. They won't be touching now but space them fairly evenly. They will puff up and join together with that lovely look of flowers in full blossom. Cover and leave in a warm draught-free place for another 1½–2 hours or so until puffed right up.

Preheat the oven to 180°C (350°F/Gas 4) and bake for about 45 minutes, covering with foil if you think it's browning too much. It's important not to overcook it or it will dry out. Cut into wedges or pull into roses when cooled.

**MAKES ABOUT 15 PIECES**

50 g (1¾ oz) fresh yeast or 21 g (¾ oz) dried yeast

125 ml (4 fl oz/½ cup) warm milk

115 g (4 oz) caster (superfine) sugar, plus 140 g (5 oz) extra

about 550 g (1 lb 4 oz) plain (all-purpose) flour

1 egg, plus 2 egg yolks

200 ml (7 fl oz) thin (pouring) cream

150 g (5½ oz) butter, softened

a pinch of salt

# HONEY TART

This is just like eating honey. The honey you use here is exactly the taste you'll end up with. I used acacia, which is very mild, but the honey pot in the restaurant where I had this was clover: *'flor predominante trevo'*. The recipe is from João, who served it to me at a restuarant in the island town of San Miguel. I loved it so much that I stood outside the restaurant for an hour, waiting to ask how it was made. Finally he came out and wrote it down and I felt as if I had struck gold.

Preheat the oven to 180°C (350°F/Gas 4). Butter two 20 cm (8 inch) springform cake tins.

Put the honey into a mixer or somewhere you'll be able to mix it with a hand-held blender. Add the butter and a bit of the milk slowly and purée. Add the rest of the milk and then the flour, and slowly and quickly purée so it is well mixed but not gluey. Pour into the tins and bake for 35–40 minutes, until the tarts are nicely browned and have left the sides of the tins. Slice when cool.

CUTS INTO ABOUT 24 SMALL RICH SLICES

500 g (1 lb 2 oz) clear runny honey

200 g (7 oz) butter, at room temperature

250 ml (9 fl oz/1 cup) milk

300 g (10½ oz) cake flour or plain (all-purpose) flour

# YOGHURT & SEMOLINA SYRUP CAKE WITH ROSEWATER

This is a very typical, and very sweet, Cypriot cake. You can leave out the rosewater and make a plain syrup-drenched cake, or add lemon juice, vanilla extract or orange blossom water to the syrup.

Preheat your oven to 180°C (350°F/Gas 4). Grease and flour a 22 cm (8½ inch) square cake tin. Cream the butter and sugar together in a large bowl with electric beaters. Whisk in the yoghurt, rosewater, egg yolks and lime zest. Sift in the flour, semolina and baking powder and mix well to incorporate. Mix in the ground almonds. In a separate bowl, whisk the egg whites until they are white, fluffy and just making soft peaks. Carefully fold these into the mixture so that they are well incorporated. Pour the batter into the tin and bake for about 45 minutes, or until the cake is deep golden and cooked through. Leave to cool while making the syrup.

To make the syrup, put the sugar, rosewater and 250 ml (9 fl oz/1 cup) of water in a small saucepan and boil for about 5 minutes. Pour the hot syrup over the cake and leave it to cool completely. To serve, cut the cake into small pieces and serve with a not-too-sweet ice cream.

SERVES 20

125 g (4½ oz) butter, softened

230 g (4¾ oz) caster (superfine) sugar

250 g (9 oz) natural yoghurt (not too thick or thin)

1 tablespoon rosewater

3 eggs, separated

½ teaspoon grated lime zest

125 g (4½ oz) plain (all-purpose) flour

125 g (4½ oz) fine semolina

2 teaspoons baking powder

55 g (2 oz) ground almonds

**ROSEWATER SYRUP**

230 g (4¾ oz) caster (superfine) sugar

1 teaspoon rosewater

# VANILLA CAKE

I love this mattressy and soft cake. Here it is plain with a beautiful white icing, but on occasion you could slice it in half through its equator and fill it with some whipped cream and a layer of not-too-sweet jam. The kids appreciate it when I stick sweets all over the icing. Or you could make a chocolate icing and stick raspberries into that.

Preheat the oven to 180°C (350°F/Gas 4) and grease a 24 cm (9½ inch) springform cake tin. Beat the butter and sugar together very well in a large bowl. Add the eggs one at a time, beating well after each one goes in. Add the vanilla and then sift in the flour and baking powder. Beat well, adding the cream or milk a little at a time. You will have a thick and creamy batter. Scrape it out into the cake tin and bake for about 45 minutes, or until a skewer poked into the centre comes out clean. Leave to cool completely before icing.

For the icing, put the butter into a bowl and gradually beat in the icing sugar. Add the vanilla and 2 tablespoons of milk and beat well, then slowly beat in the rest of the milk, stopping when you have a smooth but fairly stiff icing. Gently spread it all over the cake — it doesn't have to be perfect.

**CUTS INTO 10–12 SLICES**

250 g (9 oz) butter, softened

250 g (9 oz) caster (superfine) sugar

3 eggs

1 teaspoon vanilla extract

290 g (10¼ oz) plain (all-purpose) flour

1½ teaspoons baking powder

185 ml (6 fl oz/¾ cup) thin (pouring) cream, milk or buttermilk

**ICING**

100 g (3½ oz) butter, softened

200 g (7 oz) icing (confectioners') sugar

1 teaspoon vanilla extract

about 3 tablespoons milk

# ~ INDEX ~

Published in 2014 by Murdoch Books, an imprint of Allen & Unwin.

Murdoch Books Australia
83 Alexander Street
Crows Nest
NSW 2065
Phone: +61 (0) 2 8425 0100
Fax: +61 (0) 2 9906 2218
www.murdochbooks.com.au
info@murdochbooks.com.au

Murdoch Books UK
Erico House, 6th Floor
93-99 Upper Richmond Road
Putney, London SW15 2TG
Phone: +44 (0) 20 8785 5995
Fax: +44 (0) 20 8785 5985

For Corporate Orders & Custom Publishing contact
Noel Hammond, National Business Development Manager, Murdoch Books Australia

Publisher: Diana Hill
Design concept: Miriam Steenhauer
Design and layout: Miriam Steenhauer and Sarah Odgers
Photographer: Manos Chatzikonstantis
Stylist: Michail Touros
Editor: Katie Bosher
Project Editors: Livia Caiazzo and Katie Bosher
Production Manager: Karen Small

Text copyright © Tessa Kiros 2014
The moral right of the author has been asserted.
Design copyright © Murdoch Books 2014
Photography copyright © Manos Chatzikonstantis 2014

A cataloguing-in-publication entry is available from the catalogue of the National Library of Australia at www.nla.gov.au.

A catalogue record for this book is available from the British Library.

Colour reproduction by Splitting Image, Clayton, Victoria.

Printed by 1010 Printing International Limited, China.

IMPORTANT: Those who might be at risk from the effects of salmonella poisoning (the elderly, pregnant women, young children and those suffering from immune deficiency diseases) should consult their doctor with any concerns about eating raw eggs.

OVEN GUIDE: You may find cooking times vary depending on the oven you are using. We have used a fan-forced oven in these recipes. As a general rule, set the temperature for a conventional oven 20°C (35°F) higher than indicated in the recipe.

MEASURES GUIDE: We have used 20 ml (4 teaspoon) tablespoon measures. If you are using a 15 ml (3 teaspoon) tablespoon add an extra teaspoon of the ingredient for each tablespoon specified.

# RECIPES COLLECTED FROM THE FOLLOWING BOOKS: